Informing a nation

HORACE GREELEY

Britannica Bookshelf—Great Lives for Young Americans

Informing a nation

HORACE GREELEY

by Edward Allen

Illustrated by Robert Boehmer

Published by
BRITANNICA BOOKS
a division of
ENCYCLOPAEDIA BRITANNICA, INC., *Chicago*

TABLE OF CONTENTS

This book is for
Kevin and Brian

Chapter 1

On His Way

Across the New England countryside a tall boy walked in the spring of 1826. The air was still crisp, but the frost on the ground soon would be gone in the bright April sunshine. It was a day of hope, a day of promise, with winter well behind and summer ahead.

The boy kept a careful pace toward East Poultney, Vermont. Behind him stretched the 12 miles he had come from his home in West Haven. If the journey had tired him at all, his pace did not show it. He walked with the same determination as when he had closed his father's gate hours before.

In East Poultney he went to the office of the town newspaper, the *Northern Spectator,* and asked to see its editor, the Reverend Amos Bliss, a Baptist minister. He was told to go to the editor's home. The boy nodded his head quietly as he listened to directions.

When he arrived at the editor's home, he found him busy

working in his yard. The man did not look up as the boy came near him and stood quietly for awhile, trying to think of the right thing to say. At last, when it seemed Dr. Bliss would never notice him, the boy cleared his throat nervously and spoke.

"Are you the man that carries on the printing office?" The boy's shrill voice betrayed his nervousness.

"Yes," Dr. Bliss said. "I'm the man." He turned to look at the boy. Before him stood a tall, thin boy whose thinness made him seem even taller and more angular than he really was. He looked perhaps 14 or 15 years old with pale blond hair that was almost white and light blue eyes that were solemn and kind. His trousers were too short and Dr. Bliss could see he wore no socks. The editor looked again at the boy's eyes, and this time they met him squarely and without fear.

"Don't you want a boy to learn the trade?" the boy asked.

"Do *you* want to learn?"

"I've had some notion of it."

"It takes considerable learning to be a printer, my boy." Dr. Bliss paused. "Have you been to school much?"

"No," the boy said, "I haven't had much chance at school, but I have read some history and a little of most everything."

"Where do you live?"

"West Haven, sir."

"How did you get here?" Dr. Bliss was becoming interested.

"I walked over."

Dr. Bliss was silent for a moment. "What's your name?" he asked at last.

Now when the boy spoke, the shrillness in his voice carried with it a strength that would not soon be forgotten.

"Horace Greeley, sir."

So began the most spectacular career in the history of journalism. From his first job as a printer's apprentice in East Poultney, Vermont, Horace Greeley rose to become one of the most powerful men in America. As the founder and editor of the New York *Tribune,* his writing influenced the people's thoughts and actions as no man's had before or has since. The fame of his newspaper spread throughout the country and even to Europe. Even now his magnificent advice, "Go west, young man, and grow up with the country" is well remembered and a valuable part of our national heritage.

Horace Greeley was much more than a journalist. He was a politician as well, a molder of opinions, a critic of life in 19th century America. He was all these because he was a journalist with a mission: to build the United States into a great nation, to unify it—the East and West, the North and the South—so that it could achieve its destiny of democratic greatness.

The United States was still a young nation when Horace Greeley was born on his father's farm near Amherst, New Hampshire, on February 3, 1811. Horace was the first child; three sisters and one brother came later. His mother, Mary Woodburn Greeley, named him Horace because she had read the name in a book and decided she liked it. Soon the name was shortened to Hod. A little later, because of his nearly white blond hair and complexion, the nickname "Ghost" was given to him. This nickname followed him throughout the rest of his life.

Young Hod's father was Zaccheus Greeley, a jovial little

man with sandy-colored hair and whiskers, who was known as Zack. A happy man in those days, Zack lived the life of the rest of the farmers around Amherst. He worked hard and enjoyed the neighborhood gatherings, the cornhusking parties and country dances.

Mary Woodburn Greeley was an ideal companion for Zack. She too worked hard, helping her husband in the fields, singing happily as she handled her pitchfork with as much skill as a man. She was a strong woman, plump and with a great vitality for work or play. In the evenings, with the long day ended, she would sing or read to her children. Life was hard in New England in the early 1800's. Later, Horace Greeley wrote that his family knew "genuine poverty—not beggary, nor dependence, but the manly American sort."

That young Hod Greeley developed a keen interest in books from this life of "genuine poverty" is amazing. But he did. By the time he was three years old, he had learned to read a little. By the time he was four, he could read everything that came his way. He was sent into Londonderry to stay with his Grandfather Woodburn and attend the nearby school. Hod lived with his grandfather during the winters until he was eight years old. Then his parents decided he was big enough to walk the mile and a half to the Amherst school. Besides, his father needed him to help with the chores.

Altogether, Horace went to the district school only 45 months over a ten-year period. Finally, when he was 13, a teacher confessed that Horace knew more than he did and could just as well stay home. Already young Horace had read the Bible from beginning to end, the *Arabian Nights, Pilgrim's Progress,* and Byron, Burns, and Shakespeare. His fame as a student spread and prompted several family friends to offer to pay his way through Phillips Exeter Academy. But Zack Greeley proudly refused the offer. "Hod will have all the schooling we can afford," he said, "and that will be enough for him to get along on." It was.

Meanwhile the shadows of financial disaster were lengthening until they completely overcast the happy Greeley home. The panic of 1819 had been a severe blow to all New England. Then, in 1820, disaster finally struck. "My father and mother," Horace Greeley later wrote, "were hard-working people but poor managers. Father had a proud spirit and always wanted to entertain. He was too fond of the smiles of great men." The sheriff appeared one day and seized most of the family possessions. Zack Greeley was forced to flee into the woods to avoid debtor's prison.

Zack went on to West Haven, Vermont, and found a job chopping wood. In midwinter of 1821, he moved his family and what was left of his household things to their new home, a two-room cabin in West Haven, which he rented for $16.00 a year. If life had been difficult on the farm on Amherst, it was almost impossible in West Haven. During the rest of that first winter, Zack earned only $3.50 a week. Conditions did not improve as the years went by. He got another job clearing 50 acres of heavily wooded land at $7.00 an acre. It took nearly two years for the entire Greeley family to get it done, and even then they did not receive the full amount that was promised. They worked a farm named Flea Knoll for a while, but got no profitable return. Zack also ran a sawmill on shares. All too often there were no profits to share.

The Greeley family led a miserable existence. How they

managed was almost a miracle. "Yet," said Horace Greeley later, "we never ran into debt for anything and never were without meat, meal and wood."

All of Hod's time was spent either in school or at hard work. There was little social activity, so little in fact that once when Hod took a West Haven girl to a dance it was the talk of the town. Most of the little free time Hod had he spent reading. Just as he had done in Amherst, Horace borrowed books, newspapers, and magazines from everyone who would lend them.

Somehow Hod's interest in the printed page began to grow into a burning ambition to become a printer. When he was only 11, he and Zack walked to Whitehall, New York, to apply for a job for him. But the editor of the newspaper wanted an older boy. Hod watched all the newspapers for notice of another opening, and at last, two years later in 1826, one appeared in the *Northern Spectator*. Zack was already planning to move the family west to Erie County, Pennsylvania. Hod was determined. He decided to make the journey alone, and his father decided to let him go.

Zack never understood his son's drive to be a printer. But he knew that it was Hod's dream, and Zack had the wisdom not to interfere. On Hod's part it took all his courage to go to East Poultney, for he knew if he should get the job it would perhaps mean a final separation from his family. All these things were mixed in Hod's mind: his great desire to be a printer, the devotion he felt for his family, and the fear of living alone in a strange town.

Horace got the job. Dr. Bliss was so impressed by his honesty and ambition that he overlooked the boy's ill-fitting and shabby clothes. A week later Zack made the 12-mile trip with Hod to sign the papers required for a boy to go to work so young. Hod's salary for five years was to be room and board only for the first six months plus $40 a year thereafter for clothing. To Hod these terms seemed more than generous.

Even so, Hod was sad. While his dream of getting a job as a printer had come true, his family was still moving to Pennsylvania, a distant place that must have seemed to Hod like the other side of the world. Young Hod watched sadly as his family packed for the journey to Erie County. For a little while he forgot how much his new job meant to him, how much he had wanted it. As the time neared for his family to leave, he could think of nothing but the loneliness he would have to face with everyone that he loved far, far away.

He watched with his sad blue eyes, waiting and hoping for his mother to say only one word about his coming with them. But she did not, for she knew it would be best for her oldest son to follow his ambition. It was a heartbreaking decision for her to make, but she said goodby to her boy and gave no hint of wanting him to come to Pennsylvania with them. When Horace Greeley was grown, he admitted that if his mother had only said the word, he would joyfully have forgotten the job and gone with his family. He said much later that his walk back to East Poultney was "one of the slowest and saddest" in his life.

No doubt it was difficult. But Hod Greeley did not turn back, no matter how much he wanted to do so. If there were tears, he blinked them away and kept his eyes on the horizon.

Horace Greeley was on his way.

Chapter 2

A Great Decision

The young printer's apprentice fell to work with zeal and eagerness. His job at the *Northern Spectator* trained him to be a pressman as well as a printer. First Hod Greeley learned to set type, putting each letter in succession in a "stick" he held in his hand. Then, on the days the *Spectator* was published, he spent part of his time cranking the old flat-bed press and feeding the sheets of paper into it to be printed. He enjoyed setting type—putting together the words that would later be printed in the paper.

Like everything before, life in Poultney was hard for Hod. Even after he had been working on the *Spectator* for some time he was still wearing the same patched and worn-out clothes. One day when a fellow apprentice asked him why he didn't buy some new ones, Horace replied, "Because I have no money to pay for them and I won't go into debt."

In the evenings, Hod enjoyed reading the "exchanges"—newspapers from other places sent in return for copies of the *Spectator*. He also enjoyed arguing local and national politics. These pastimes, along with reading in the local public library, offered a chance for Hod to continue his education. His only recreation was walking. He went on long hikes, oftentimes to another village or perhaps to some spot he had heard about and wanted to see. Usually he would take along a book or two as his only companions.

Hod Greeley's serious approach to his work was soon rewarded when Dr. Bliss allowed him to condense the news from the large city newspapers for use in the *Spectator*. Later, when the editor had to leave East Poultney for a few days on business, young Hod was given authority to prepare stories for publication. For the first time, the words of Horace Greeley —whose words later on would shake the entire nation—began to appear in print.

Fortunately, Greeley's journalistic influence did not remain limited to the subscribers of the *Northern Spectator*. In the spring of 1830, the owners of the newspapers decided that it could never be made profitable and that the only thing to do was to stop publication. The decision, of course, left young Hod without a job.

With nothing definitely in mind, Hod set out on foot for his family in Pennsylvania. During two previous summer vacations he had visited them on their four acres of land in the western forest of the state. Their home was a log cabin, and there was little joy in it with the tall trees hiding the sun for all but a few hours each day. Horace, surveying the situation, saw the discouragement of his father and mother, brothers and sisters. His mother, particularly, was broken by the hardships of pioneer life.

Disturbed by his family's plight, Hod determined to do what he could to help. He worked a few weeks with Zack, helping clear more land. Then he found a job in Jamestown, New York, as a typesetter on the *Journal*. He planned to send most of his salary to his family, but his employers at the *Journal* decided it would be more economical to owe him his wages!

So, disappointed, Hod returned to the log cabin. He remained there until January, 1831, when another job opened up for him on the Erie *Gazette*. The owner, Joseph Sherrett, was so impressed with the young man that after only five months Hod was offered an interest in the paper.

It was a tempting offer, indeed, but apparently Hod Greeley already had other things in mind, for he turned down Sherrett's offer and announced his intention to move to New York City. "Upon full consideration," he later wrote, "I decided to turn my steps toward the Commercial Emporium while still considerably younger than I would have preferred to be on making such a venture."

Horace Greeley never explained the decision any further than that. Sherrett's offer in 1831 should have seemed to Hod Greeley the ultimate peak of success. Certainly, it would have helped his family immensely. Even so, the Hod Greeley of 1831 was a different young man from the untested youth of 1826. Spending the rest of his days in Erie, Pennsylvania, was clearly not enough for him.

That he had any notion of the heights to which he might later rise is uncertain. But that he left for New York City with confidence is sure. After a final visit to Erie County, where he

[*19*]

left all but $25 of his savings, Hod Greeley set out for the "Commercial Emporium."

Getting there was an adventure: hiking, picking up a day's work when he could along the way, moving on to another town, sometimes on foot, sometimes on a barge. Through the Mohawk Valley he went and from Albany on down the Hudson River on a boat towing canal barges. On August 17, 1831, the buildings and houses, the wharves and many-masted mer-

Young Hod Greeley saw New York City as a brave new world.

chant ships of New York City came into view.

New York neither knew nor cared when Hod Greeley first stepped ashore and entered it. He was a tall, gangling youth of 20. His shabby clothes and shuffling walk carried no hint as he walked along, peering at the vastness of the city, that his would be the most powerful voice in its history.

Chapter 3

On His Own

T he New York City to which Horace Greeley came in that summer of 1831 was a bustling, growing young metropolis of 200,000 people. Of all these, Horace Greeley knew not one. He walked the streets, still with his red kerchief bundle of clothes on his shoulder, and marveled at the city's hugeness.

In those days the city did not even cover the full 12-mile length of Manhattan Island. Thick woods and a few farms lay between the Hudson and East Rivers. In the city itself a four-story building was quite a landmark. Even so, it was all new and magnificent to the 20-year-old printer. The houses were brick and stone instead of the rustic frames and log cabins of East Poultney and Westhaven. There were even mansions that seemed more wonderful to Horace Greeley than anything he had ever imagined.

It was a rowdy town as well, with vaudeville and fireworks at Niblo's Garden on Broadway. Violence raged in the thickly populated area east of the Bowery. There mobs terrorized the population on election days, fights broke out in the streets every day, and criminals went unchecked and almost unnoticed. The city was too busy growing to notice.

But if parts of New York were ugly, other parts were beautiful. The city was beginning to attract world wide attention for its great business activity, its tremendous growth, and its expanding culture. By the time Greeley arrived in 1831, New York had surpassed Philadelphia as a literary center. From time to time a romantic young man named Edgar Allan Poe stormed into town, his black military cloak swirling around his shoulders. Across the East River in Brooklyn a youth named Walt Whitman was beginning to write poetry. Already another great poet, William Cullen Bryant, was the editor of the New York *Evening Post*. Seldom has a city of 200,000 people had so many outstanding men.

The problem at hand for Horace was to find a place to live and a job. Of the $25 he had when he started his trip to New York, only $10 was left. He found a room for $2.50 a week and began searching for a job. For several weeks in August he walked the scorching, hot streets and found nothing. Finally, when he was almost ready to give up, a man in his rooming house told him of a job he might be able to get in West's printing shop. The next day Horace appeared early to apply.

The foreman was unimpressed with the gangling youth. Though Horace had spent almost $5 on a new suit of clothes, it did not help much. The shop did need a journeyman printer, however, and the foreman decided to give Horace a chance at setting type.

It was a difficult and exacting task. The foreman gave Horace the most difficult copy he could find, with many technical words and phrases which are always dangerous pitfalls for a typesetter. To make the test even harder, Horace was told to set the copy in pearl and agate type, the very smallest in the shop. Worst of all, the copy was to be set in columns about half the width of a newspaper column. The job looked impossible, but Horace did it and landed his first job in New York.

Later in the day, the owner noticed Horace at work and asked his foreman why he had hired the odd-looking young man.

"He's the best I can do."

"Well," said Mr. West, "pay him off tonight and let him go."

But they kept Horace Greeley, because at the end of the 12-hour day Horace had set the copy with very few mistakes. Most of what Horace had set was ready to be printed.

During the next year and a half Horace Greeley worked in New York as a journeyman printer, setting type 14 hours a day for $6 a week. He lived in cheap rooming houses and ate in the most economical places he could find so that his living expenses were about half of his $6 weekly paycheck. He learned well what it meant to be a poor workingman in a large city. And he never forgot it.

Throughout the slow-marching months, Horace Greeley's reputation spread. In the print shops he became known as a hard and fast worker. If he seemed a bit odd in dress and manners, it was all right because he also seemed to be something of a genius. He was keenly interested in politics and could talk for hours on the subject. His mind was alert and he usually won arguments. He continued to read every book and newspaper that came his way. This reading and discussion led Horace to admire the great United States Senator from Kentucky, Henry Clay. In 1832, when Horace was old enough to vote in his first Presidential election, he cast his vote for Clay. But "Old Hickory," Andrew Jackson, won in a Democratic landslide.

Despite young Greeley's seriousness, he was also known for his great wit and good nature. Though he saved his money carefully, he lent it generously—just as he had in East Poultney —to anyone he felt was deserving and in real need. Unfortunately his judgment was not always the best. In a little over a year he had lost $60 of his hard-earned pay by lending to people who never paid him back.

One of Horace Greeley's last employers, J. A. Redfield, said of him late in 1832: "He was queer in looks and queer in his ways, but he was the best printer we ever had." Though young Horace did not know it at the time, he was nearing the end of working for other men. Soon he would be on his own.

Earlier, Horace had become friends with Francis V. Story while they were both working on a popular paper, the *Spirit of the Times*. Story had been foreman of the shop while Greeley was a journeyman printer. As they worked together, Story came to admire the tow-headed young man's skill and intelligence. So, when Story had a chance to open his own print shop, he thought of Horace Greeley.

Story approached Greeley and explained that he had been promised all the printing of the *Bank Note Reporter*, a weekly magazine, as well as the printing of a new daily newspaper, the New York *Post*. Story's offer was the opportunity for which Greeley had been waiting. They each invested $100 in the business, got credit for $40 worth of type, and the printing firm of Greeley & Story was launched. The type foundry extending credit to them was the only one in the city willing to take a chance on them. In appreciation of their confidence, Greeley eventually bought $50,000 worth of type for use on the New York *Tribune*.

The guarantee of printing both a weekly magazine and a daily newspaper was a bright beginning for the young printers. Their hopes received a severe jolt, however, when, after only a few weeks of publication, the New York *Post* went out of business. The *Post* had been conceived as a "cheap-for-cash" daily, the first of its kind in New York and possibly in the world. When its first edition appeared on New Year's Day of 1833, it sold for two cents a copy. Two weeks later the price was lowered to a penny a copy, and it began to sell. But unfortunately, the publisher's financial resources were gone by then.

Greeley & Story struggled along, printing the weekly *Bank Note Reporter* with Greeley setting all the type for it himself. Slowly, the business began to prosper and they accepted even the smallest printing jobs, ones that the larger printing shops in New York would have turned down. By the beginning of summer Greeley and Story's fortune was looking up. In July, Story drowned in the East River. Shortly thereafter, his brother-in-law, Jonas Winchester, took up Story's half-interest in the firm, and it moved forward again.

Horace Greeley had come remarkably far in such a short time. But even this was not enough to satisfy him, and he started thinking of bringing out a magazine of his own. He did not rush it. For it was not Horace Greeley's nature to let his ambition become the driving force of his life.

He never tried to push himself ahead at the expense of others. In Erie he even argued politics vigorously with everyone at the paper, and it surprised everyone when the publisher offered him an interest. When he got to New York, he worked hard for a solid year and a half as a journeyman printer; and no doubt he often wondered if he had made a mistake in leaving Erie.

But now, with his own printing business going well, he knew he had done the right thing. His savings account at the bank started to grow. Profits from the printing business were good, and he was also being paid to write editorials for the *Daily Whig* and for the *Constitutionalist*. Perhaps the writing he did for these two journals made him ask himself: "If I can write for these publications, why not for my own?"

He had read and enjoyed the *Pennsylvania Gazette*, founded in 1728 by Benjamin Franklin. He explained to his partner that he would like to establish a weekly magazine in New York City similar to it, one devoted to current literature and politics. It would be low-priced at $2.00 a year compared with $5.00 and $8.00 charged by competitors, the *Knickerbocker* and the *North American Review*. The profits, Greeley stated, would come from the printing business, and it would not be necessary to invest more money to start the magazine. Winchester and a new partner, Sibbett, listened and finally agreed to begin the new magazine.

The first issue of the *New-Yorker* came out on March 22, 1834, and within a few issues the genius of Horace Greeley as a publisher became apparent. He had been a good printer and had written excellent editorials for others. He had read widely and had developed a keen sense of what makes good writing.

It was Greeley who first spotted the work of an English writer named Charles Dickens. At the time he was almost unknown in England and was writing under the pen name Boz. Greeley found one of his stories in an English magazine and reprinted it in the pages of the *New-Yorker*. Greeley was also one of the first supporters of Edgar Allan Poe. Several of his first pieces appeared in the *New-Yorker*. "Poe is a brilliant writer . . ." said Greeley. History has proved him right. As with Dickens, Greeley made his own decision concerning Poe's worth as a writer without waiting for the praise of literary critics. This is characteristic of a great editor. Greeley never waited for others' approval before he put a man's work into print. Throughout his life he took great chances in hiring men, with no thought of their past accomplishment. He took his chances with many unknown writers, and many of them proved to be great.

As the editor and publisher of the *New-Yorker*, Greeley was also its typesetter, its printer, and its chief writer. When he founded the magazine, every part of its preparation was either done or personally directed by him. The composing room and editorial offices were combined into one large area so that the printer could become the editor by walking only a few feet. He and his partners had moved to an old brick building at 18 Ann Street. The offices of the *New-Yorker* could be reached only by climbing a dark stairwell with worn-out wooden steps that threatened to give way at any moment.

When the first issue of the *New-Yorker* came out, there

was not a single subscriber. But its reputation for quality spread quickly, and subscriptions promptly started coming in at a rate of 100 per week. By September, the *New-Yorker* had 2,500 paid subscribers. Happily, Greeley showed the list to his two partners, who were still interested only in the printing end of the business. Cautiously, Winchester pointed out that it was fine to have so many readers—but when was the young magazine going to show a profit?

That question Horace Greeley could not answer. To him, it did not seem important. As long as the printing business was good, the *New-Yorker* could continue. This was enough to make him happier than he had ever been before.

Winchester and Sibbett watched as their senior partner went back to his desk with his odd, lurching walk, proudly stuffing the circulation list into his pocket. They looked at each other and shook their heads sadly.

They left him in a little while, putting out all the lights except the one he was using. They paused and looked once more at Greeley, his white hair shining in the single light beside his desk. His pen moved quickly across a sheet of paper. Neither of the men asked Greeley if he was ready to quit for the day. They knew he was not.

Chapter 4

A Man Comes Calling

The circulation of the *New-Yorker* rose steadily. Contributors such as Dickens and Poe brought in more subscribers each week. Certainly not the least of the *New-Yorker's* attractions were Horace Greeley's editorials. More than any journalist before, Greeley had a way of putting thoughts into words that interested and excited readers.

Throughout his early years of reading, Horace Greeley developed his own ideas. By the time he founded the *New-Yorker*, there were very few subjects he had not studied. And, as his readers soon learned, when Greeley had studied something he made up his mind about it quickly. He was always ready to let everyone know his opinion. His interests ranged wide, from agriculture to philosophy and religion. He was especially interested in literature and politics.

The middle 1830's—when the *New-Yorker* first appeared —were interesting years. Politics was a lively subject and no one had a livelier time talking and writing about it than Horace Greeley.

At the time, there was really only one political party, the Democratic party of President Andrew Jackson. Jackson was a great man and a great President of the United States, but just as happens today, there were many people who disagreed with him. Horace Greeley was one of them. Greeley felt that Jackson's administration was too strong, that the government was involved in too many activities. Greeley believed that established methods were best and that they should not be changed until it was absolutely certain that a change would be an improvement.

Greeley was clearly against slavery in the South, or in any state, and he wrote vigorous editorials against it. At the same time he never believed in trying to solve the problem by violence. Another subject he wrote about was the question of a high or low tariff. Greeley was always in favor of a very high protective tariff, a tax on goods made in foreign nations and sent to the United States to be sold. Greeley felt foreign competition was unfair to U.S. manufacturers and workers.

All these attitudes worked together to make Greeley sympathize with the political party that was just beginning to rise against President Jackson's strong Democratics. This party was the Whigs. The party was headed by Daniel Webster and Henry Clay. And it was supported vigorously by Horace Greeley.

The circulation of the *New-Yorker* continued to climb. Within two years it reached 5,000. It was an interesting, exciting magazine and its influence in the literary and political world was growing. No longer was its young, white-haired editor to be taken lightly—or brushed off with a smile of amusement. At last he was beginning to be recognized as a serious and gifted editor.

But if the *New-Yorker* was becoming a force, the profit sheet did not show it. True, its circulation was growing, but in the publishing business, a large number of subscribers is not enough. There must be a good amount of advertising if a publication is to do well.

Greeley fought desperately to keep his magazine going. One night he wrote: "I paid off every one to-night. Have ten dollars left and have to raise $350 on Monday. Borrowing places all sucked dry. I shall raise it, however." It was a bad situation and Greeley knew it. His partners were beginning to complain more and more about the continued losses of the *New-Yorker*. He knew that something would have to be done. He also knew he would never give up as an editor and return to the simple life of a printer.

Finally the partnership could go on no longer. Winchester was tired of the magazine's steady losses, which were always made up from the printing company's profits. Greeley was at last weary of listening to his partners' complaints. He decided to end the printing business and his partnership with Winchester. It was agreed that Greeley would take the *New-Yorker* and leave the profitable printing business to his partners. Once more, Greeley had made a hard decision, risking everything on the slim chance that his magazine would succeed.

It was 1836—ten years after Greeley had started his career in East Poultney—and he was 25 years old. It was a year of decision for Greeley and for the nation as well: Andrew Jackson's chosen man, Martin Van Buren, ran for the Presidency and kept the Democrats in the White House. Greeley decided to stay with his beloved magazine to the very end.

But in 1836, the *New-Yorker* got some stiff competition for his attention. He met and promptly fell in love with Mary Youngs Cheney. He met her at his boarding house.

The towering young editor found Mary Cheney fascinating.

She was Horace's exact opposite in appearance, with long, dark hair and brilliant black eyes. Her complexion was light and made her eyes look soft and beautiful to Horace. She was barely five feet, four inches tall and the lanky editor of the *New-Yorker* towered over her.

Horace learned that Mary was a young teacher in a private school for girls. She had come to New York in the early 1830's just as Horace had. Her home had been Cornwall, Connecticut, and she modestly pointed out to her new friend that she was 22 years old, three years younger than Horace.

During the next few weeks they continued to meet in the evenings at the boardinghouse and to see more of each other on the weekends. Horace learned, perhaps to his surprise, that the young beauty was much more than just another pretty girl. She was—of all things—interested in philosophy. Here was a beautiful girl who loved to sing and laugh and dance—and who also loved to think. It was a combination Horace Greeley could not resist.

Just as their romance got under way, Mary accepted another teaching job in Warrenton, North Carolina. When she was gone, Horace felt completely alone in the world. It was not a new feeling, but now that he had found Mary he could not stand it. They wrote to each other regularly and Horace waited each day for the postman to bring some word from his sweetheart.

Horace found it almost impossible to think about the *New-Yorker,* literature, politics, or anything else but the dark-eyed girl he had grown to love so much. Then, in the summer, he reached his decision. He wrote Mary a long letter, asking her to marry him.

Horace left New York City for Warrenton, North Carolina, and there, on July 5, 1836, he and Mary Youngs Cheney were married at the home of Squire William Bragg. Greeley chatted with his host, Squire Bragg, and the Squire mentioned that his son, Braxton Bragg, was a student at West Point. Later,

Braxton Bragg was a general in the Confederate Army. Wherever Horace Greeley went, fate brought him in contact with important people. For a journalist, there could be no better luck.

The Greeleys returned to New York City and rented a place at 124 Green Street near the Battery. Far from being in the best residential section, it was at least near Greeley's office. Mary did not mind the lack of luxury, for they were rich in friends and had good times together. As the custom was in those days, Mary began having "Friday-at-homes," casual parties attended by all the literary people in New York. The conversation was always an adventure for the serious young beauty who was now the wife of a well-known, if not yet famous, New York editor. Publishers, writers, editors, professors, all came to the modest Greeley home, and they were charmed by Horace's beautiful and intelligent wife. In turn, she was flattered by their attention and compliments. It was an exciting life for both of them. They went to lectures and concerts, sometimes walking in the chilly fall evenings. As winter came, their home was a warm place in spirit as well as fact.

Greeley was unbelievably happy as the *New-Yorker* circulation shot near the 9,000 mark, making it the largest literary magazine of the time. It was even making a little money. Life was happy as 1836 came to a close, and the serious young editor actually danced the quadrille at a Christmas Eve party.

But the happy times did not last long. In 1837 the nation was hit hard by depression. The subscription list of the *New-Yorker* fell to 6,000, with many subscribers not paying regularly. Once more, money worries beset Horace Greeley. His

[*34*]

home was no longer modest; it now was simply poor. The *New-Yorker* lost even more as the months dragged on. For the first time, Horace Greeley began to feel that bankruptcy was just around the corner. He was saved, however, at the last moment by a $1,000 loan from Dudley S. Gregory. Greeley took the money thankfully and paid his most pressing debts— and kept on fighting to save his magazine. It was a hard fight. He began writing editorials again for other publications, but the pay was not enough to help very much.

Winter came and things were no better. Still Greeley fought on, setting his own type and printing the *New-Yorker* himself. Then, on an especially raw and unpleasant morning, Greeley trudged slowly up the steps to his office. It was cold inside and he left his coat on. Slowly—and sadly—he began setting type, wondering how many more weeks he could last.

Downstairs, and unknown to Greeley, a well dressed man was walking along the street, looking for the office of the *New-Yorker*. He paused before the old, dirty brick building. Then he turned his hand on the doorknob and entered. Before him was the dark stairwell leading to the *New-Yorker* office. Slowly the man started up the steps—on a mission that would change the course of Horace Greeley's life entirely.

Chapter 5

"Weed, Seward, and Greeley"

H orace Greeley stood in a lonely corner of the large room that served as the *New-Yorker's* plant and office. He was busy setting type for the next week's issue and did not look up.

"Is the editor here?" the man asked.

Greeley put his work down and looked to see who it was.

"I'm Thurlow Weed," the man said. "I'd like to see the editor of the *New-Yorker*."

"I'm Horace Greeley." He moved forward, and the tall visitor extended his hand.

"I'd like to discuss securing your services as the editor of a campaign paper we are going to publish in Albany," Weed said.

Greeley looked at Weed, perhaps wondering if he were dreaming. Greeley knew him by reputation, a fellow journalist, the editor of the Albany *Evening Journal*. Long ago, when Greeley had hiked to his parents' home in Pennsylvania, he passed through Rochester, New York, and read Weed's editorials in the *Telegraph*. Greeley never dreamed then that in a few years he too would be an editor, and that Weed would be calling on him. They sat down at Greeley's desk and talked.

Their careers were similar, except that Weed was a little older and a little further along in the publishing business. But they had worked in many of the same towns as journeyman printers in the Mohawk Valley before Weed had settled in Albany and Greeley in New York. They talked shop for a while, with Weed feeling out the younger editor to be sure he was the right man for the job.

Weed was as much a politician as he was a journalist. When the Whig party had been organized, he established himself as the most powerful member of the party in the state of New York. His purpose was to have his favorite, William H. Seward, elected governor. There was much work to do, for the Democrats would fight hard to keep control of the state. Weed knew he would need help—that he could not possibly run the Whig party in New York and edit both his newspaper and a new campaign paper. He had read many of Greeley's editorials in the *New-Yorker* and was convinced he would be the ideal editor of the campaign paper.

After their talk in Greeley's office, Weed felt even surer that he had found the right man. Only one thing stood in the way: Greeley stated flatly he would not give up publishing the *New-Yorker* and move to Albany. Weed might have gone to another man. But he liked Greeley very much and did not want to give up. He invited Greeley to dine with him that evening at the City Hotel.

Greeley went, and found Thurlow Weed had also invited

Lewis Benedict, chairman of the Whig State Committee. The three men talked for several hours. Greeley finally won. The Whig leaders agreed to his coming to Albany for three days each week to edit the campaign paper. The remaining days would be his own to return to New York City and edit his magazine. Weed offered Greeley $1,000 for a year's work and hinted that the salary could be much higher if Greeley would come to Albany on a full-time basis. But of course, Greeley refused. He was his own man, as he always had been. The three men parted late in the evening with the details of the campaign paper finally settled. Even Horace Greeley's suggestion for a name, the *Jeffersonian,* was accepted.

It was another hard decision: to stick by his own *New-Yorker* and work for the *Jeffersonian* only three days a week. Like most of Greeley's decisions before it, the price paid for it was high. Immediately he advertised in the *New-Yorker* for a partner who could help him. He was still in debt, and selling part of his interest in the magazine seemed the quickest way to remedy the situation. There were a few replies to his advertisement, but no one was seriously interested in a business that was already losing so much money. Each month the *New-Yorker* was taking in about $500 while the costs were running to $1,000. It is easy to see why Greeley had such trouble in finding a partner.

But he would not give up. "Give me all the time you can, my friend," he wrote to Thurlow Weed in Albany, "and I will turn the corner yet." And turn it he did. The first issue of the *Jeffersonian* appeared on February 17, 1838. The schedule Greeley set for himself was enough for any other three men.

Miraculously, Greeley convinced W. Matlack Eldridge

and Elbridge G. Paige to join him as partners in the *New-Yorker*. They later proved unsatisfactory, but for the present it was better than nothing. Having two partners allowed Greeley to leave New York each Saturday night on a boat for Albany. After an all-night trip, he usually arrived in Albany early Sunday morning. He lived at Weed's home.

Weed described Greeley's visits well: "He would arrive from the boat two hours before breakfast with his pockets stuffed full of newspapers which he would diligently read until summoned to [the] table." As soon as he finished breakfast, Greeley went to the *Journal* office, where he began working on the *Jeffersonian*. Usually he finished writing it in three days, and it was ready for printing on Tuesday. After another 150-mile boatride, Greeley arrived at the *New-Yorker* office on Wednesday morning with just enough time to get it out by Friday afternoon. On Saturday, he planned the next week's *New-Yorker*, then caught the night boat again for Albany.

That Horace Greeley worked and lived on such a schedule is almost unbelievable. But he did. He even found time to write a few editorials for other publications! These pieces brought only about $12 a week on an average, but every extra penny was needed to keep the *New-Yorker* in business. Many editorials, of course, were written in support of Seward, the Whig candidate for governor. He read one of Greeley's editorials in the Fredonia *Censor* and wrote about it to Weed: "Make my acknowledgement to H. G. for that beautiful article in 'The Censor.' I have never seen anything better turned out or in better temper or more discreet."

As usual, Greeley was having far from an easy time. Editing two publications 150 miles apart was a severe strain.

There was simply too much to do and too many troubles. During the winter, the Hudson River was closed with ice, and he was forced to remain in Albany most of the time. The *New-Yorker* was left in poor hands, and he worried a great deal about it. When the ice finally broke and the river was clear enough to travel, Greeley hurried to New York. It was probably for this trip that Horace Greeley bought the first of his famous white overcoats, with large pockets on the sides that could be stuffed with newspapers and magazines and many notes to remind himself of things to be done.

At home, Mary Greeley was expecting her first child, and Horace wanted very much to be able to stay with his wife. The *New-Yorker,* he discovered, was in worse financial shape than ever. His new partners had made several mistakes. His literary critic had quit, and Greeley was not able to persuade him to come back. Then, on a Wednesday morning in August, Horace Greeley returned from Albany to find that his first son had been born but was dead. He went straight to his wife's bedside. She was still desperately ill. She was a tiny, frail woman, and it was six months before she was able to get out of her sickbed.

Greeley wrote, and the state of New York read and believed him. The circulation of the *Jeffersonian* rose to 15,000 copies. This, along with Greeley's editorials in his own *New-Yorker* and other publications, was a deciding force in the election of Seward.

Writing of his father's victory, Frederick Seward later remarked: " 'The Jeffersonian' and 'The New Yorker' were favorite journals of the Whig families, and the editor was regarded as having great ability, great industry, much eccentricity, honesty, singleness of purpose, and of no particular ambition save in his own profession." Greeley's great contribution was seen by Weed as well as Seward. The two politicians began to think of the young editor as their "junior partner" in the control of the Whig party of New York State.

With the election over—and won for Seward—Greeley could see no sense in continuing the long trips away from his invalid wife. Weed tried to talk Greeley into continuing the *Jeffersonian,* but the weary editor had had enough. In February of 1839, the last issue was published, and Greeley ended one of the most difficult, and most successful, periods in his life.

The panic of 1837 had almost broken Horace Greeley and the *New-Yorker.* By 1839, things were no better. True, he had been saved by a loan from a friend, then by the investment of two new partners, then finally by the $1,000 salary from Weed. Times had been hard for Greeley, and one result was a dramatic change in his political thinking.

Before the 1837 panic, Greeley had been completely conservative. He felt that the only functions the federal government should have were to keep order and see that justice was done in private disputes. But as hard times dragged on, hurting not only Greeley but thousands of others, he realized that the government had a greater obligation: the well-being of the people. He urged such liberal ideas as the distribution of $75,000,000 in treasury notes among the states, and he suggested a $5,000,000 program of "internal improvements" to relieve the depression. From 1837 on, Horace Greeley favored a more active government, one that would try to do the things which individual citizens could not do for themselves. The nation was growing and there was much that needed to be done.

There was poverty in the East and opportunity in the West. Greeley recognized both and filled every issue of the *New-Yorker* with advice to settle in the West. "Fly," he wrote, "scatter through the country, to the great west. It is your true destination! If you have no family or friends to aid you here turn your face and hope to that fertile land. . . ." In other editorials he asked such questions as, "What Shall We Do For The Laborer?" and explained his program of work-relief. From that time on, Horace Greeley fought for a country that would be a better place in which to live.

But Greeley's own world in 1839 was far from good. His financial struggles continued. The $1,000 salary from Weed no longer came to him, his wife was still in bed and showing few signs of recovery, and his debts were climbing ever higher. He took a job at $12 a week editing the New York *Whig* and he continued writing editorials for other publications. To a friend, he wrote in June of that year:

"I am getting along so-so—working confoundedly hard and existing on $12 a week, which I could do very easily and fatly if I had not every sort of call upon me. For instance, I have spent this week's salary already and not one sixpenny of it . . . to my own advantage or belly. Yours in great trepidation, H. G."

Meanwhile, Weed and Seward were busy in Albany. Weed, the master politician, was looking ahead eagerly to the national election of 1840. His ambition was to see a Whig elected President. He could hardly be bothered with his friend Greeley's problems. Greeley did not ask for any help; nor was it offered.

Before the Whigs met in national convention in December

of 1839 at Harrisburg, Pennsylvania, Weed remembered his "junior partner" in New York, and asked Greeley to attend it with him. Weed convinced Greeley that his long-standing favorite, Clay, could never win the election. At the convention, Weed, Seward, and Greeley managed to stop Clay's almost certain nomination. But they were unable to nominate their own candidate, General Winfield Scott. Instead, their second choice, William Henry Harrison was nominated. The Clay forces were furious. To soothe them the convention nominated a strong Clay supporter, John Tyler, for vice president.

Weed and Seward realized the job of winning New York's vote in 1840 would be difficult. The Democrats had renominated President Van Buren, and Greeley was needed in Albany again to edit another campaign paper. They invited Greeley to Albany to discuss the problems of the campaign. They hoped to persuade Greeley to re-establish the *Jeffersonian*. But as might be expected, their "junior partner" had other ideas.

Even though he needed money desperately, Greeley drove a hard bargain with his politician friends. He agreed to edit a new campaign weekly to be called the *Log Cabin*. Instead of taking a salary, he wanted to own the paper. Weed realized that the "junior partner" was developing a mind of his own a little too fast, but he had to agree. On May 2, 1840, the first issue of Greeley's *Log Cabin* appeared.

Within nine weeks the editorial blasts from Greeley's pen had carried the new paper's circulation to 56,000 copies, and as election day came near, circulation zoomed to 80,000. The paper published a song each week and was always aimed at the masses. The aim was good, for Harrison swept to victory and became the first Whig President.

Once more, Greeley had made a valuable contribution to the Whig party. And once more Weed and Seward did not bother to thank him. Weed kept busy running the political affairs of the Whigs in New York; Seward was again in the governor's mansion and his political star was burning bright. Greeley, on the other hand, was still hopelessly in debt with the added burden of the *Log Cabin*. With the election over, circulation of the new publication dropped to only 10,000. The *New-Yorker* continued to lose money heavily despite its reputation as the nation's leading literary magazine.

At home Horace Greeley had nursed his wife back to at least delicate health, only to receive the cruel blow of another sickness and the death of another baby. The year 1840 closed quietly. The Greeleys' life was calm even if it was not entirely happy. Mary was not well, but Horace was cheered as she slowly seemed to improve. The drop in the *Log Cabin's* circulation finally leveled off and the paper began to show a tiny profit. "I am beginning to feel quite snug and comfortable," he said to Weed during the winter.

Even the heartache of the *New-Yorker* was lessened as a capable and brilliant young man named Henry Jarvis Raymond went to work for Greeley. Mary Greeley continued to feel better. The *New-Yorker* steadily improved. Greeley had some time to think and even some time to dream. Deep in his heart and in his mind the dream began to come to life.

He called it by a simple name: the New York *Tribune*.

Chapter 6

The New York Tribune

Horace Greeley dreamed of a daily penny newspaper in New York City that would reflect his own progressive Whig views. Already the *Sun* and the *Herald* were selling for a penny and making money. The *Herald* proudly claimed an annual income of $130,000, and Greeley could see no reason for the *Tribune* to do less. Besides, the promise of advertising from important Whigs in New York City seemed to make certain the new paper's success.

But Greeley had little to recommend him as a daily newspaper publisher. Except for writing occasional editorials, he had no experience with the trials of putting out a paper every day. The battle of a weekly publication is hard; it is exactly seven times harder with a daily. Launching such an ambitious project was even more difficult with the competition of four other morning newspapers.

The prospects of success were not bright, but certainly

they were as good as the *New-Yorker*'s when it was launched. Greeley proceeded with his plans to start the *Tribune*. James Coggeshall, a New York Whig, lent him $1,000, and Greeley himself had about $2,000, half of it in printing equipment.

With financial arrangements made, Greeley planned to put out the first edition of the *Tribune* on March 4, 1841, William Henry Harrison's inauguration day. Unfortunately a delay in getting the necessary mechanical equipment forced a postponement. But on April 3, Greeley printed a card in the *Log Cabin* announcing that the *New York Tribune* would publish its first issue on April 10th. The very next day, April 4, President Harrison died after only a month in office. The first day of publication for the *Tribune,* was the day of mourning for the President in New York City. It was a bleak, chill day with sleet falling from the dark grey skies. Horace Greeley had printed 5,000 copies of the first issue, but 500 would probably have been enough. The young publisher, now 30 years old, was not encouraged.

On April 11, however, the *Tribune* was on the street again. The clouds lifted, the paper sold, and Greeley felt a little relieved. The *Tribune* has continued to the present time while its competitors, who seemed so large in 1841, are either out of business or—like the *Herald* and the *Sun*—now a part of Greeley's great paper.

From the beginning, the magic of Greeley's editorial genius made the *Tribune* popular. As with all his earlier publishing efforts, circulation grew steadily until it reached 10,-000 paid readers in a year. If Greeley was an editorial genius, however, he was a failure at business management. By July, the *Tribune* was following the same pattern as the *New-*

Yorker: soaring gains in circulation were exceeded only by the large money loss. Promised advertising from the Whig supporters did not come; and Greeley knew that without it his paper would eventually fail.

What hurt the most was the absence from the advertising columns of the powerful Clay-supporting Whig merchants. They knew that Greeley was the "junior partner" in the political firm of Weed, Seward and Greeley, and that Weed was responsible for Clay's defeat in the Whig convention. Weed and Seward again did nothing to help Greeley. They could have influenced many Whig advertisers, just as they had promised to do. But they were silent, the Whig merchants advertised in other papers, and Greeley was too proud to complain about broken promises.

After a month's publication, Greeley wrote Weed: "I am getting ahead very well but thus far I have not had $30 of advertising from Whigs as such, though I expected more. I don't want to beg any of it, but I shall have a hard fight to live through the summer without some help of the kind. . . ." Still help did not come from Weed or Seward. As they learned later extremely well, Greeley did not forget.

Within another month Greeley realized that the burden of running the business of the paper was more than he could manage. Handling the *Tribune's* editorial columns was a huge task, and he needed a partner to look after the paper's advertising and business problems. On June 10, he wrote to a friend in Philadelphia: "I am poor as a church mouse and not half so saucy. I had losses this week, and am perplexed and afflicted. But better luck must come. I am fishing for a partner."

By the end of July he had found his man, Thomas Mc-

Elrath, a lawyer who also had publishing experience. For $2,000 Horace Greeley sold him an equal ownership of the *Tribune*. Immediately McElrath began bringing in the Clay-Whig merchants, slowly at first, but finally in large numbers. He put the management of the paper on a business-like basis, and the *Tribune* began to make money.

In the fall, the *New-Yorker* and the *Log Cabin* were merged into a new edition of the *Tribune* that was designed to appeal to readers outside the New York City area. It was called the *Weekly Tribune* and it quickly gained a circulation of 15,000. By the end of the first year, both the daily and weekly editions were showing a steady profit. Gone at last—and forever—for the young white-haired editor from New England were the miserable days of poverty and awful indebtedness. At last he had time to concentrate on the one thing he loved most in this world: publishing his newspaper.

During the next few years the people of New York, the United States, and the world saw sweeping changes in journalism made by Greeley's *Tribune*—changes that altered permanently the traditions of newspaper publishing. No less important were the many progressive campaigns Greeley fought and won. He was one of the first to argue for a shorter work week, one of the first to recognize labor's right to organize itself into unions, and he was the president of the first printer's union. He sold his newspaper stock to those whose work he admired; he was the father of the "profit-sharing plan" as it is known today. Always, he used the editorial page of the *Tribune* to argue for what he believed was right.

One key to Greeley's quick success as the publisher of a daily newspaper is found in his partner, Thomas McElrath.

Greeley knew that he needed help and he recognized that his own judgment in business matters was not the best. He searched until he found the man he wanted to be his partner. His choice was excellent.

It was the same with the editorial staff. Time after time, Greeley brought in men other papers would have turned away. Time after time, the men who worked at the *Tribune* were later praised as the best newspapermen in the world.

One of these was Henry J. Raymond, who had joined Greeley in the *New-Yorker* days. Greeley liked the young Vermonter very much and admired his ability and talent. When the first edition of the *Tribune* appeared, Greeley put the line, "Assisted by H. R. Raymond" at the top of the editorial page. Raymond was an unknown youth only a few months out of college at the time. The act of confidence was justified, for Raymond later became the editor of the New York *Times* and even served as lieutenant governor of the state.

A young newspaperman, Bayard Taylor, who later became famous as a critic for the *Tribune,* decided to come to New York City. He wrote a letter to the great poet-editor of the New York *Evening Post,* William Cullen Bryant, asking for a job. Young Taylor's experience was not enough for Bryant, and he dismissed him with a short note. Greeley, on the other hand, told him, "I'll try you for six weeks." At the end of the trial, nothing was said; so Taylor kept on working. Finally, after he had worked three months, Greeley spoke to him. With no fanfare, Greeley told the young man he had been doing a good job and deserved a vacation. When Taylor returned, his salary had been raised.

A few years later Bayard Taylor received one of the most

historically important letters even written by a newspaper editor. On January 13, 1849, Greeley wrote to him:

"Dear Bayard:

I must not defer to thank you for your article on Pope Pius IX the other day. It was very well done indeed. I wish you would resolve henceforth to write one such article per week, and sign your own initials or some distinguishing mark at the bottom. I want everyone connected with "The Tribune" to become known to the public as doing what he does.

H. G."

In this one short letter much of Greeley's greatness as an editor can be seen. In a few sentences, he shows a full grasp of the secret of editorial greatness: before a man can become a great editor of books, a magazine, or a daily newspaper, he must become an editor of men. Greeley understood this better than anyone ever had before. And no one ever has better understood it since. His offer to have Bayard Taylor sign his articles in the *Tribune* was historic. Never before had a "by-line" appeared in a daily newspaper. It had never occurred to an editor to give his writers the rich reward of personal recognition until Greeley did it in 1849.

Still, Greeley was a hard man to work for, especially if a mistake were made in a story. He had little patience with blunders, and he could change from a happy, smiling mood into fury when he found factual error in a reporter's story. His voice pierced to every corner of the *Tribune* office when "the old man" got angry. With all fairness, however, if the same reporter who made the mistake one day managed to do a good job the next, Greeley would be the first to tell him so, to compliment him, and to tell him to "keep up the good work." It was not easy to work for Horace Greeley, but if a man did a good job, there was not a better newspaper in the world.

More than anything else, the *Tribune* was Horace Greeley's. From his arrival each day around noon until his departure at midnight or later, Greeley ruled his paper with an iron hand. All policies were established by him—nothing was done without first having Greeley's approval. "For whatever is distinctive in the views or doctrines of the *Tribune* there is but *one* person responsible," he wrote. That *"one* person" was Horace Greeley.

Chapter 7

Writing for the Common People

As the first year of the *Tribune* came to a close, it was still published in the old Ann Street building that had been the home of the *New-Yorker* and the *Log Cabin*. More space was taken as more was needed, but few real changes were made. The building was still old and dirty, giving no hint of the lively, new paper published inside its ugly walls. McElrath's brilliant business management was stealing advertisers from the other New York papers while Greeley's genius was stealing readers. The publishers of the *Herald,* the *Post,* the *Courier,* and the *Enquirer* all were worried, for every day the *Tribune* became stronger and more powerful. No longer did the competitors joke about the upstart newcomer.

And no longer did they joke about its unusual editor. For Greeley attacked them all, made jokes himself, and hurled biting insults. The competitors responded. It was just what Greeley wanted. When the readers of the *Herald,* for example, read James Gordon Bennett's editorials raging in hot fury against the *Tribune's* editor, what was more natural than for readers to want to see for themselves why Bennett was so angry? What did they do to find out? They bought the *Tribune*! Greeley poured it on—and circulation soared.

For his own part, though, Greeley was the same. Only now he took a little pride in his peculiarity. He described himself as a tow-headed, half-bald, slouching, long-legged man "so rocking in gait that he walks down both sides of the street at once." He still wore the old white coat, now a personal trademark, with its pockets bulging out until they were almost bursting with papers, magazines, notes, and books. "People suppose I wear the same old coat," Greeley said to a friend. "But I don't. The original white coat came from Ireland. I bought it from an immigrant who needed money and I needed a coat."

As editor, Greeley kept in close touch with the print shop.

Such was Horace Greeley in 1842. Now established as a leading New York editor, he had no need to apologize to any man. He used the editorial columns of the *Tribune* as had never been done before. Time after time he hammered away at what he thought was wrong and praised what he thought was right. A good example of Greeley-in-action was his attitude toward President Tyler, the Whig vice-president who became President after Harrison's early death. In the beginning of Tyler's administration, Greeley urged the people to give the new President a chance to prove himself. "Let us hear him first," Greeley wrote, "and then judge." Nothing could have been fairer. Greeley and the nation waited, heard, and finally judged.

Tyler moved quickly, showing the entire nation that he was not to be pushed around by the Whig party that had elected him. He vetoed an important bill of Henry Clay's—and Greeley began to fear that President Tyler was showing a dangerous amount of independence. But this was all, for Greeley himself was always independent and never accepted an idea because it was the official Whig viewpoint. In the *Tribune,* Greeley's criticism of Tyler was mild. He reminded his fellow Whigs: "We can destroy Whig supremacy, we may break up the Cabinet, but we cannot depose President Tyler."

A little later Tyler vetoed another bill, one dear to Greeley's heart: the protective tariff bill to prevent foreign competition. Greeley's reaction was far from mild this time: "Treason is lurking in the Capitol . . . " and "a Judas [Tyler] engaged in a conspiracy to defeat the overwhelming desire of the country that Clay should be elected President in 1844." With this, Greeley made it plain he would not support Tyler for re-election. Greeley's support was ended forever.

In many ways, Greeley's decision on Tyler was hasty, for the tough-minded President had much in his favor. There was great expansion in the West, to Oregon in the Northwest and Texas in the Southwest. Much of this excitement over the West can be credited to Greeley's own editorials since the old *New-Yorker* days. Now, with the nation clamoring for expansion to include these vast areas, Greeley opposed Tyler's policy to bring the independent Republic of Texas into the Union. In a great and dramatic statement, a young Congressman from Illinois, Stephen A. Douglas, said: "The two oceans are our boundary fixed by God." President Tyler agreed, the people of America agreed, and in the last days of his administration Congress voted to offer admission to the Union to the Republic of Texas.

In Greeley's battle with Tyler there was a strong element of party politics. Tyler had abandoned his own Whig party, and had set out alone on what Greeley himself once called "the boiling sea of politics." In putting his veto on the protective tariff, Tyler shut himself out of the Whig party. But because he was a Whig, the Democrats wanted no part of him either. Actually, his views on expansion of the United States were closer to the Democratic policy than to his own Whigs. But Tyler had taken his position and had to stand the consequences. Through most of his years in office he was a President without a party. Fortunately, the people were with him even though the politicians were not. For Greeley's own part, it must be remembered that the protective tariff was one of his favorite ideas, and he could never forgive Tyler for killing it. Also, United States expansion to the West could also mean an ex-

[58]

pansion of slavery, a social injustice Horace Greeley had always fought.

President Tyler was not the only subject of Horace Greeley's fiery editorials. As the *Tribune* built a solid financial basis, Greeley was able to attack anything he felt was wrong. One thing he felt was wrong was the relation of businesses to their workers. For any man to be at the complete mercy of his boss, Greeley felt, was bad. The working man had a right to work, to earn money for his family. The depression following the panic of 1837 had left many unemployed, with no place to go, no one to ask for help. It was an evil situation and Greeley meant to do something about it. Quickly he was criticized for his protection of the mass of working-people. Quickly he responded:—"Let them work twenty years as hard as I have done and feel and know the hopelessness of the great mass of laborers, the emptiness of their lives, the dullness of their few leisure hours as I do before they attempt to lecture me."

Greeley was not sure what the solution to the problem might be. Albert Brisbane finally convinced him that the solution was a theory called Association. Brisbane's idea came from his own study of a French philosopher of the time, Charles Fourier.

Briefly Association suggested that workers should organize into small "communities" of 500 to 2,000 people, all working in either agriculture or industry, and sharing in the profits according to each man's value to the group. The important thing, to Greeley, was that in Association every man would have a job, every man would have a fair paycheck for his efforts. It was a way to solve the awful problem of poverty and Greeley immediately began arguing for it on the editorial pages of the New York *Tribune* and the *Weekly Tribune*.

Several communities of the Association type were organized. Within 15 years all had failed because of a lack of sound business management. Even so, the idea of a community in which every man had a job—with no trace of poverty—always remained a goal for Greeley. Impossible though it might be, he wanted desperately to remove from the nation anything and everything that was bad. And he never gave up. Thirty years later, the town now called Greeley, Colorado was established on much the same lines as the Association communities of the 1840's.

In addition to the Whig national policies and the rights of the laboring-man, Horace Greeley fought for a variety of other things, including equal rights for women.

It was a dangerous position for Greeley to take. The other New York newspapers were against all rights for women. And when Greeley sent a reporter to cover a convention of women suffragists in Worcester, Massachusetts, the other newspapers laughed at the *Tribune* and even published cartoons showing Greeley in a woman's dress! But Greeley held firm and published his reporter's stories of the women's convention. Calmly he made the other editors eat their words with a truly great editorial on the subject of women's right to vote: ". . . when a sincere republican is asked to say in sober earnestness what adequate reason he can give for refusing the demand of women for an equal participation with men in political rights, he must answer—None . . . ."

The *Tribune* was a very young paper when these editorial blasts were issued. Each was written in opposition to very powerful forces. Many feared Greeley would ruin his newspaper if he did not calm it down. Weed, especially, was worried and began urging the "junior partner" to run the *Tribune* more conservatively. Greeley heard the complaints and answered:

"If anyone would prefer to discontinue 'The Tribune' . . . we beg them not to delay one minute on our account. We shall all live till it is our time to die, whether we earn a living making newspapers or by doing something else."

Thus Greeley let everyone know that the *Tribune* was his paper and would be run in whatever way he thought best. To make the matter completely clear to Weed, Greeley wrote him a letter in February, 1842, just before the *Tribune's* first birthday. ". . . I will not ask you to think as I do," Greeley wrote. "I only want a chance to think for myself."

His partner, McElrath, worried about where Greeley's ideas might eventually lead their young daily newspaper; and he urged Greeley to slow down a bit. But Greeley was on his way, and so was the *Tribune*. McElrath could not argue with the circulation figures, for people were reading the *Tribune* and beginning to believe in it.

The initials, "H. G." at the bottom of an editorial were looked for every day, because the people sensed that the writer was speaking with honesty and from the depth of his heart. Here was something unusual, something they had not seen before in a newspaper: an editor who was speaking to them, the people, about the things that were important to them. And he spoke in a simple way, a way they could trust. Greeley himself explained it: "Writing for the common people, I have aimed to be lucid and simple. I· write for the great mass of intelligent, observant, reflecting farmers and mechanics, and if I succeed in making my positions clearly understood I do not fear that they will be rejected."

Chapter 8

Making the Tribune Great

As Horace Greeley and his *Tribune* rounded out the first early years of success, he turned his attention to the coming Presidential election of 1844. Greeley was still an active Whig, and he was still thought of as the "junior partner" in the political firm of "Weed, Seward and Greeley." But the "junior partner" was not entirely satisfied with his status. During 1842, Weed had gone too far in his criticisms of Greeley and the *Tribune*. Finally, Greeley decided to make it plain that if a "partnership" existed at all, Greeley was now a "full partner." He wrote Weed on September 10, 1842:

"Friend Weed:

I rise from a bed of sleepless thought to make plain my position to you. I trust it is now understood, as I thought it had been before, that we differ radically on the Bank bill and I begin to fear we do on the general policy and objects of political controversy . . . .

I cannot realize that there have been any series of obligations between us which render it proper in you to assume so complete a mastery over my opinions and actions . . . .

I have given you, and I have been ever ready to give you, any service in my power, but my understanding, my judgment, my consciousness of conviction, of duty and public good— them I can surrender to no man. You wrong yourself in asking. However deep my obligations I cannot pay in these. I am ever ready to defer to your superior experience and judgment— only convince me, but do not assume to dictate or lecture me. Do not ask me to forget that I, too, am a man—that I must breathe free air or be stifled.

Let us now hope that we understand each other better. I would hope also that we may still be friends; but if I can only enjoy your friendship on terms of humiliation, let us be strangers henceforth . . . . While I remain where I am I cannot afford to despise myself. Besides, I owe what little chance for usefulness that I may have to the impression that I do no man's bidding but speak my own thoughts.

Horace Greeley"

Few men have spoken their "own thoughts" more clearly. With this letter Greeley resigned as "junior partner." On an equal basis, the three continued for several years to be active in the Whig party of New York. But without question, Weed would not have accepted such a letter from the Greeley of the *Jeffersonian* or *Log Cabin*. This Greeley was different: he was the editor of a powerful newspaper in the state's largest city. Weed had no choice but to take him on his own terms.

So, with the political firm patched up, the three men moved together once more, this time to try to get Henry Clay elected President of the United States. They traveled to Baltimore for the Whig Convention, and Clay was nominated on the first ballot by acclamation. The Whigs felt victory was certain with Clay. He was famous and respected, even idolized by many. Since his defeat for the Presidency by Andrew Jackson in 1832, he had conducted himself in the United States Senate in a way that even his foes admired.

The *Tribune* and Greeley could not have been happier: "Of Clay's nomination not a word need be said. [The decision] had been virtually made a long time since by one million and a half Whig voters." And the *Tribune* predicted ". . . he will be elected by an immense majority of the people."

But the people favored expansion to the west—they were in favor of taking the Republic of Texas into the Union by treaty—and Clay was against it. The Democrats in convention surprised the Whigs by nominating James K. Polk of Tennessee—and calling him "Young Hickory." They campaigned on a platform favoring expansion in the West and the annexation of Texas. It was a staggering blow to Clay, to the Whigs, and to Horace Greeley. With his usual honesty, he told the *Tribune's* readers that a long and hard fight was ahead.

During the campaign no one worked harder than Greeley. In the first Presidential election since the *Tribune* had been founded, Greeley meant for his newspaper to have a part in the victory. He worked desperately, writing, making speeches, attending rallies whenever and wherever he could. He even published another paper, the *Clay Tribune*. The *Tribune* itself blazed with editorials praising the Kentucky senator and calling James Polk a "third-rate politician" and "a catastrophe."

But nothing helped. The issues were clear and the people

[*65*]

voted for what they wanted. The name of Clay was great in the nation, and his opponent was unknown by comparison. Still the people wanted expansion to the west and the annexation of Texas. They voted their desire and Clay was defeated.

In many ways it was a great and progressive election; for the nation stirred from its quietness and moved on to the West and greatness. But for the moment, it was the saddest of times for Clay and Greeley. Writing of Clay's loss, Greeley said: "I have admired and trusted many statesmen but I profoundly loved Henry Clay . . . . He was more fitted to win and enjoy popularity than any other American who ever lived."

Clay's defeat was made even worse for Greeley because it was the first time since he had been an editor that the Whig candidate had lost. With the *Jeffersonian*, Greeley had helped elect Seward governor of New York. With the *Log Cabin,* Greeley helped Harrison win the Presidency. In both cases, Greeley was sure the Whig candidates were the best men available; but in no sense of the word could they be compared with Clay. Greeley's interest in Clay's campaign was personal. When Clay lost, Greeley took it as a personal defeat. Sadly, he turned his attention back to the day-to-day operation of his newspaper —and to his life at home with Mary.

The Greeleys still lived in rooming houses near the *Tribune* office in the poor part of Manhattan. During the first years of their marriage, they had moved around quite a bit and it had not mattered to either of them. But in the 1840's they quit making so many moves and began to think of finding a permanent home.

From 1840 on, Horace Greeley's burdens were increased by the many complaints of his wife Mary. He was patient with her, however, and she responded to his care. She was never well—or at least never thought she was—but she did maintain some kind of a normal home for her hardworking editor-husband. He was away much of the time, and when he was at home he was always thinking about the *Tribune*. Horace Greeley was not an easy man to get along with, and it is no wonder that Mary often pretended illness just to get a normal amount of his attention. It must be remembered that she stuck close to him through all the miserable years of poverty in their early married days. In turn, Horace did not forget it, and he seldom complained when his frail little wife was in a sickbed for months at a time. Theirs was not a happy marriage in the usual sense, but Mary and Horace Greeley were close in spirit. As it turned out, Mary was more responsible than any other person for many of the great writers who came to work on the *Tribune*.

In 1844 Mary was at last feeling better. In March a son had been born to them, Arthur Young Greeley. They gave him the nickname "Pickie." He was a fair-skinned baby with blond hair just as his father had been before him. He immediately became the great joy of his parents' lives. Mary, especially, planned her entire world around their "golden boy." Horace began to think more and more of a permanent home for his family, a better place than the crowded New York streets for Pickie to grow to manhood. He discussed it with Mary and she agreed. She even felt that getting out of the rooming house might improve her health.

Horace finally found a house he thought would make a good home for his family in an area called Turtle Bay about two miles up Manhattan Island from New York. There were many trees on the eight-acre plot of land and there was a wonderful view of the East River. The house had not been lived in for many years and was in extremely poor condition when the Greeleys bought it. The location, however, was beautiful, and Horace yearned for a return to the country life he had known as a boy. It was impossible for him to consider anything in the city home. He had lived there for 13 years, but it still seemed strange to him. He turned to the woods and hills of northern Manhattan Island quite naturally.

The Greeleys had a house at Turtle Bay, but they never had a real home. Mary Greeley paid little attention to anything except Pickie. Greeley himself was busier than ever at the *Tribune* because his talented assistant Raymond had left to work for the *Courier* and *Express*. The full weight of the paper's editorial department was on Greeley's shoulders. More and more, Greeley had to be away from his new home in order to keep a sharp eye on the *Tribune*. Mary could find little reason to work hard at homemaking for a husband who was gone so much. The only transportation was a two-horse stagecoach, which ran every hour until 11 at night. Often, the *Tribune's* weary editor would have to remain at the paper until past midnight to see that a story got in on time, that there were no mistakes, and that the paper would be printed correctly. When he was through, the last stage often would have left for Turtle Bay, and Greeley would have no choice but to spend the night in the city.

It was a hard life for Horace, and it was just as hard for his wife. Mary worshiped their young son, but she also wanted companionship with people her own age. Fortunately, she turned at last to the group of thinkers in New England known to the world as the transcendentalists.

Mary had always been interested in philosophy, literature, and education. In the early 1840's she became friendly with one of the famous transcendentalists, Margaret Fuller. By the time Pickie was born, Miss Fuller was one of the Greeleys' closest friends. She was a brilliant woman, the first editor of the *Dial*, and a close associate of the leaders of the transcendentalism movement, Ralph Waldo Emerson and Henry David Thoreau. Mary enjoyed her "summers-in-Boston" immensely and finally persuaded Horace to come with her to meet these interesting people.

It might have seemed fast company for someone of Horace's limited education, but it was not. Greeley's mind was as quick as any of the intellectuals he met, and they accepted and respected him. He developed a strong and lasting friendship with Margaret Fuller. With Thoreau, Greeley made arrangements to act as his literary agent in New York. But it was at Brook Farm that the New York editor gained the most for himself and for the *Tribune*.

Brook Farm, organized by George Ripley and a group of other transcendentalists, was located near Roxbury, Massachusetts, as an experiment very similar to the Association theory that Greeley already admired. The chief difference was that Brook Farm was composed of intellectuals, while in Association, the communities were mostly workers. The aim of Brook Farm was to enrich the mind and soul; the aim of "Association" was only to prevent poverty. But the fundamental idea was very similar—a group of people living and working together for the benefit of all.

Greeley felt the Brook Farm system was not quite practical

enough. He argued the point with Ripley, Miss Fuller, and another Brook Farmer, Charles Anderson Dana. On the other hand, Association seemed lacking to the Brook Farmers in an all-important ingredient called culture. This, Greeley would argue, was a matter of individual choice. If one wished to spend time reading books, there was certainly nothing in Association that would prevent it.

Their talks continued and Greeley made a lasting impression on the Brook Farmers. Eventually, they all accepted his ideas. In 1846, Dana even accepted a job on the *Tribune* as its city editor. Later he became the first journalist to hold a title invented by Horace Greeley—managing editor. Dana's career as the *Tribune's* managing editor and much later as the editor of the New York *Sun* was only another example of Greeley's wisdom in selecting good men for his newspaper.

Greeley and Dana made an odd combination. Greeley was the "Man in the White Coat"—peculiar in appearance, persuasive in conversation, powerful in writing. Dana preferred the quiet life of books and ideas. Dana was a great man and a great editor, but he was the exact opposite of Greeley. Dana was a thinker, and Greeley was a man of quick and decisive action. Strangely enough, though, the two men got along well together, and therefore made the most potent editorial team the newspaper profession had ever seen.

They worked together for 16 years on the *Tribune*. Sometimes their views were the same; at other times they differed entirely. Dana, for instance, insisted that anything that happened was fit to be published in the *Tribune*. For a change, Greeley held the conservative view. He felt the *Tribune* should use judgment in what it passed along to its readers.

Raymond and Dana both learned the newspaper business from Horace Greeley. In their own right, these two men became great journalists themselves. If Greeley had made no other contribution than bringing these two into the profession, his reputation would still be great. Both acknowledged their debt.

Raymond, who parted with Greeley on rather unfriendly terms, at least stated that the *Tribune's* editor "decided the whole course" of his life. Raymond was always at odds with his employer in the *Tribune's* many editorial campaigns. When Raymond left Greeley, he carried much anger with him—and he never lost it. They worked together only briefly, to be sure, but there is no doubt of Greeley's influence on the man who became the great editor of the New York *Times.*

Dana was more eloquent on his debt, probably because he and Greeley worked together much longer and were much closer friends. In explaining Greeley, Dana gave one of the best summaries ever written of how a newspaper should be edited:

"Every man who has charge of a newspaper, who controls a newspaper, has to have a moral code by which he is guided in the conduct of his own paper. In order that I might not state it inaccurately, I have noted down what I conceive to be the professional code that governed Mr. Greeley:

" 'Always give a hearing to your opponent. Never attack a man and refuse to let him answer in the same columns. Be always as considerate of the weak and friendless as of the powerful. Waste no strength in advocating that which is . . . impossible. Never compromise your own opinions on account of your subscribers. If they don't like your ideas they can always go to another shop.'

"That was the doctrine of Horace Greeley; and that doctrine he practiced during the whole of his active life. I cannot remember, amid all the controversies (and they were often very bitter controversies) in which he was continually engaged, that he ever violated one of those principles."

As Dana expressed it, the "professional code" of Greeley is the standard that has made newspapers great. Dana's remarks about Greeley's code of journalism are just as useful today as they were in Dana's time.

Brook Farm yielded even more than Dana to the *Tribune*. Miss Fuller, Mary Greeley's first friend in the Brook Farm group, and Ripley both came to New York to work on the *Tribune*. Miss Fuller established the *Tribune's* "literary department," and Ripley became one of the newspaper's most respected writers and critics. Along with Dana, also a brilliant writer, the *Tribune* brought together in a few short years the most amazing staff in the history of the United States. Not a single New York newspaper, including the *Post* with William Cullen Bryant as its editor, could compare with the *Tribune*.

In 1845 a new Tribune Building was erected at Nassau and Spruce Streets after fire had destroyed the old Ann Street building. The new building was not mortgaged; the *Tribune's* rapidly increasing profits paid for it. The new presses and all the paper's mechanical equipment were the best available. In furnishing the office, however, Greeley and McElrath were less particular. In their opinion it did not matter what sort of chairs were available; it was who sat on them that counted.

Greeley filled them first with such writers as Dana, Miss Fuller, and Ripley, all from Brook Farm. He added the traveler and poet, Bayard Taylor. Miss Fuller's "literary department," an experiment in newspaper publishing, gave *Tribune* readers more than "just the news." Her column was widely accepted and gave the *Tribune* new dignity. Greeley broadened the concept of newspaper publishing to include intelligent, critical articles on art, music, and science. Miss Fuller sailed for Europe in August of 1846 but continued to send occasional articles to the *Tribune.*

Greeley awaited her articles eagerly, and so did the *Tribune's* rapidly increasing number of readers. Greeley also waited for her letters to him and his family, for Margaret Fuller had become the Greeleys' closest and dearest friend.

When she had first agreed to come to New York City and write for the *Tribune,* she also had insisted that she live with the Greeleys at Turtle Bay. She wanted no part of life in New York, and she did not feel that she would be able to write well if she did not have just the right surroundings. It annoyed Greeley to have her in his home. He was further annoyed when she informed him that her articles would not appear on a "regular" basis—that she would submit them when they were ready and not before. As a daily newspaperman, Greeley could not understand such artistic temperament. Still, he agreed, and waited patiently for her articles to come to his desk.

Unhappily, Greeley tolerated her presence in his home. But Mary loved her companionship, and Pickie adored his Aunty Margaret. Eventually Horace learned to admire and love her as much as his wife and Pickie did. She was a strange woman and very difficult to understand. But when she finally left Turtle Bay in 1846 to go to Rome, the ancient city she had always loved, the Greeleys knew the best friend they had ever had was gone.

[73]

During the next few years she and Greeley exchanged many letters. His told of life at Turtle Bay, the long days of hard work at the *Tribune,* but most of all they told the story of Pickie and their new baby, a little girl born in November of 1846. Greeley's first letters were happy ones, for as 1846 ended, all seemed brighter than ever before in his life.

Chapter 9

Politics, Progress, and Power

The Man in the White Coat, as the *Tribune's* editor already was known, turned the corner into 1847 with a rush. The *Tribune* was breaking its own circulation and advertising records. With Dana and the other "Brook Farmers" on its staff, the newspaper's prestige grew with each day's edition. Particularly, Greeley's editorials gained more and more readers for the *Weekly Tribune*. Greeley, as always was at his editorial-best when writing about political affairs. Editorial writing in the 1840's emphasized politics as it does today. Greeley was deeply involved and concerned with politics, and politics had much to do with the *Tribune's* early and lasting success. It was the force behind Greeley's drive to the top as a newspaper publisher.

Greeley continued to write vigorous articles proposing free land in the West for settlers. The campaign did wonders for the *Weekly Tribune's* circulation in the West. But his editorials opposing slavery lost as many readers in the South as were gained in the West and North. The fires of the slavery question were beginning to flame high in both the Whig and the Democratic parties. The *Tribune* left no question in anyone's mind about where it stood.

The Democratic party, especially, was suffering from serious divisions. Texas had been brought into the Union under Democratic President Polk—and war with Mexico had broken out as a result. In settling with Mexico, Polk asked Congress for $2,000,000 to use in negotiation. To this appropriation bill a Democrat from Pennsylvania named David Wilmot attached an amendment that became known as the Wilmot Proviso. It provided that no territory acquired from Mexico would allow slavery. The amendment was defeated, but it split the Democratic Party into warring groups: those opposed to slavery and those in favor of it. When Congress adjourned, the Whigs felt their position was improved by the Democratic split. True, the Whigs were split on the same question; but the Whigs were out of power, and the thirst for victory in 1848 held them together.

The Democratic convention in Baltimore nominated Lewis Cass, who was opposed to the Wilmot Proviso. Cass favored "squatter sovereignty" to solve the slavery problem. This doctrine proposed that those who settled the West should decide for themselves whether or not to allow slavery in their territories.

The Whigs named General Zachary Taylor as their candidate for President when they met in Philadelphia. Taylor had little to recommend him except that he had become a national hero in the recent Mexican War. And he was available.

The Whigs did not even bother to write a platform.

Greeley attended the Whig convention and fought hard against Taylor's nomination. First, he supported Clay for another try at the Presidency; then, with little encouragement, he began to switch to John McLean of Ohio. To Greeley, anyone would be better than Taylor. To his friend Schuyler Colfax, he wrote only two months before the convention: "We cannot with any decency support General Taylor . . . . his unqualified devotion to slavery; his destitution of qualifications and principles, place him at an immeasureable distance from the Presidency . . . we may elect him, but we destroy the Whig Party . . . . I wash my hands of the business."

The Whig convention in 1848 was a clear example of power politics at work. Weed wanted Taylor as the candidate and nothing could stop him. On the fourth ballot, Taylor was nominated. With great disgust, Greeley returned to New York without even waiting to see who might be nominated for the vice-presidency. In the *Tribune,* he quickly branded Taylor's nomination and the entire Whig convention a "slaughter-house" of Whig principles.

Meanwhile, the convention must have felt a twinge of conscience. For vice-president, they nominated Millard Fillmore, a friend of Henry Clay. Weed fought it, but naming Taylor for President was the limit of his power. This slight defeat of the Weed political machine pleased Horace Greeley. It was not enough, however, to make him announce his support of the Whig ticket.

Throughout the summer, Greeley held back the *Tribune's* support, and even Weed became alarmed. The *Tribune* was a tremendous force in New York City, throughout the state, and in the West; and Weed knew he needed Greeley's support to win the election. In other elections Greeley had always put the name of the Whig candidate on the masthead of his paper. But as late as September, Taylor's name was still not there.

Finally, in mid-September, Greeley wrote another letter to his editor-friend Colfax. In it he said:

"I am going to vote for Taylor—at least I think I am, and I am not clear that this is right . . . .

"So I cling to a party which never loved me and am helping elect a President who will shun me. I could shake down the whole rotten fabric by a bugle-blast, yet will not sound it because some good men I love would be crushed within the ruins.

"Taylor will be elected and I, cussed by those I serve and deserted by subscribers for the most opposite reasons, shall be where 'he that doubteth' belongs! Well, who cares? . . . If the Whig carcass wins this election it will not soon win another. Mark it! H. G."

History marked it well, for Taylor was elected President on the strength of his reputation as a military hero, the last man ever elected on the Whig party's national ticket. Greeley had read the future accurately. In March of 1849 Greeley attended Taylor's inauguration. Sending his report back to the *Tribune,* he described the inaugural ball as being "so rich in glitter, so poor in feeling." He reminded his readers once more that, in his opinion, the man who should have been elected President still was Henry Clay.

Greeley returned to New York tired from so much politics and weary of trying to save the Whig party from falling completely apart. He turned his attention to his family at Turtle

Bay and to improving the *Tribune*. Greeley's life returned at last to normal. He worked long hours, and he talked a great deal with his partner, McElrath, about selling some of the *Tribune's* stock to its employees. At home, he played with Pickie and wrote long letters to Margaret Fuller. Life at Turtle Bay was quiet as winter ended and spring came again. It was a pleasant, even happy, time. The new daughter had taken part of the sting away from their first daughter's death when she was only a few months old. Pickie was growing fast, and Greeley wrote to Miss Fuller, urging her to return from Rome.

Spring warmed into summer, bringing with it in 1849 an epidemic of dreaded cholera in the city. The Greeleys were especially glad their home was no longer in the middle of what was now the epidemic area. But somehow the disease spread north until, on July 11, it struck an awful blow at Turtle Bay. Pickie, who had always been completely protected from the outside world, came down with cholera. The next afternoon he was much worse and by 5 o'clock he died. It happened quickly and without warning. Shocked almost to disbelief, Greeley wrote to his friend in Rome: "Ah Margaret! the world grows dark with us. You grieve, for Rome has fallen; I mourn, for Pickie is dead!"

But at least their baby girl, Ida Lillian, was saved from the disease and grew to adulthood. Another son, Raphael, was to be born in 1851—only to die of croup when he was six. Still another daughter, Gabrielle, came in 1857 and with her sister Ida, was strong and healthy. But the Greeleys' experience in parenthood was tragic. Of five children born, only the two girls survived. Mary Greeley was a broken woman in spirit as well as in health. Even Horace Greeley wondered if so much

[*79*]

tragedy was a punishment for his sins.

Still, life went on with what was left. The *Tribune* continued to grow. Weed ruled Whig politics with his usual firmness and skill, while Horace Greeley was sent to Congress to fill an unfinished term in the House of Representatives.

The Man in the White Coat arrived in Washington early in December and immediately went to work. Just as his editorial blasts in the *Tribune* were aimed at all the troubles of the world, his work in Congress was aimed at cleaning out everything he thought was wrong. In the short time Greeley was there, he proposed a mountain of legislation, including changing the name of the country to Columbia! He continued to support a high protective tariff, free land and homesteading in the West, and abolition of the slave trade in the District of Columbia. He also began to investigate some practices that other Congressmen would have been far happier to see him leave alone.

One of these was the amount of money paid to Congressmen for travel to and from their homes. Each member was paid an allowance for the mileage involved on the route he usually took between his home and Washington. Greeley found that his fellow Congressmen were being paid on the basis of routes that covered many unnecessary miles. Greeley compared these allowances with what the Congressmen should have been drawing for taking the most direct route to their homes. The results were amazing. For one session of Congress, $62,105.20 had been allowed in unnecessary mileage expenses. Worst of all, to the Congressmen, Greeley published his figures in the New York *Tribune*. Such exposure in one of the nation's leading newspapers was met with less than enthusiasm by Congress.

[*80*]

"Demagogue!" Greeley's fellow-representatives shouted. They reminded him that only a short time before he had voted to provide Congressmen with books for their personal libraries. There was even talk of having Greeley expelled from the House. When he rose to speak in his own defense, insults were hurled at him from all sides. "I have divided the House," he wrote "into two parties . . . one that would like to see me extinguished and the other that wouldn't be satisfied without a hand in doing it." By the time his short term in Congress was ended, he was plainly the most disliked man in the chamber.

Greeley's attempts at reforming Congress failed for obvious reasons. But his efforts to reform the New York *Tribune* were a great success. In the same year, 1849, Greeley held a meeting of his company and offered to sell as much of his stock as employees wished to buy. McElrath had not agreed to his partner's idea of profit-sharing and had decided to keep his full 50 per cent ownership. At the end of the meeting, Greeley's ownership in his own newspaper had been reduced to only a third of its stock. He firmly believed labor should be rewarded by eventual ownership. As always, he backed his belief with action.

Greeley not only offered to sell his stock, he made it easy to buy as well. He provided that each purchaser would gain immediate ownership of the *Tribune* stock, even if he did not have money to pay for it. The stock would be paid for out of its own profits, so that actually it was almost given away by the man who had worked so hard to make it valuable. Few records in the history of business can compare with Greeley's recognition of his employees.

In all, six new partners were taken into the *Tribune's* family. One of them was Thomas N. Rooker, the foreman of the composing room, where all the type was set. A little later, Greeley set aside another ten shares for Charles A. Dana—once more to be paid for out of profits. The *Tribune's* profit in 1849 was $25,000, worth much more in those days than the same amount would be worth now. Within another year, Greeley and McElrath had taken in five more stockholders, and Greeley's ownership was reduced by his own desires to just 25 percent. Here was profit-sharing as it has seldom been seen.

Nor did this end Greeley's recognition of the workers in his newspaper plant. For years, he had been working hard to improve the general conditions of labor in America. He had written thousands of words in the *New-Yorker,* the *Jeffersonian,* the *Log Cabin,* the *Tribune* and other publications to help the worker gain a more secure position. He had supported Association and had been severely criticized for it. Now, in January of 1850, Horace Greeley supported the organization of the first printer's union. Amazing as it may seem today, Greeley was supporting a labor union in his own business! The first meeting of the union was held on January 19 at Stoneall's Hotel in New York. Greeley not only attended the meeting but was actually elected the president of the New York Printer's Union. He issued and signed the first union card ever given to a printer in the United States. And he represented capital and management, as they are now known. In his new office as president of the union, Horace Greeley moved quickly to effect general improvements for the printers of New York.

Within six months after his election, Greeley accomplished more than had ever been done for New York labor in its long history of overwork and underpay. Greeley fought hard, arguing not only with the printing shops, but with the newspaper publishers as well. He insisted that there was no freedom of labor when a man is told to either work 13 hours a day or get out. For the first time, a fixed scale of wages and working hours was established. The union was organized in most of the printing shops of the city.

As the 19th century hit the midway point, there was not a more progressive editor or man than Horace Greeley. His words looked into the future, spurring the country on to greatness. His actions gave living force to the impact of his words.

Chapter 10

A Threat of War

T he *Tribune* and Horace Greeley roared together into the 1850's as one of the nation's most powerful voices. No longer was there any question about the *Tribune's* surviving. It not only was surviving—it was quickly catching up with and passing its competitors in both circulation and advertising. The question now was not whether the *Tribune* would last, but whether the others could stand the competition.

Already Greeley's *Tribune* had 200 employees, with over 100 working full time. Soon the newspaper would have 12 full-time editors, 20 correspondents in the United States, and 18 others in foreign cities. Another Brook Farmer, William Henry Fry, joined the *Tribune* staff in the London and Paris offices. Later, he became the paper's music critic.

In 1850 Greeley again showed his remarkable ability to bring outstanding talent to his newspaper. James S. Pike, a young reporter from Maine, was building a reputation for him-

self as the Washington correspondent for the Boston *Courier.*
In a typical letter, Greeley made him a mouth-watering proposition. "Will you write me some letters?" Greeley asked him.
"You are writing such admirably bad ones for 'The Courier'
that I fancy you are putting all your unreason into them and
you can give me some of the pure juice. Try! What I want is a
daily letter . . . on the doings of Congress, or on anything
spicy or interesting, letting the readers do their own thinking
rather than . . . you . . . doing it for them."

Three days later, Greeley wrote Pike again, asking him to
telegraph his stories to the *Tribune* rather than mail them.
Everyone, Greeley said, was "anxious to know what ought not
to be known, and we must get some of it in 'The Tribune' or
we will be voted dull, indolent and behind the times!" Pike
was sold. He served the *Tribune* for many years and became one
of the great political reporters of all time.

Before Pike joined the *Tribune,* however, it looked as
though he would turn the offer down. Dana had been trying
for some time to hire him and had even gone so far as to hint
that the *Tribune* would give him some stock in the paper. Dana
pointed out that the profit had risen from $25,000 in 1849 to
$50,000 in 1850, and 1851 seemed a cinch to hit between
$40,000 and $60,000. Pike was impressed, but not interested.
Greeley persuaded him on more professional grounds. The
nation and Congress were slowly showing signs of a violent
controversy over slavery. No one knew, including Greeley,
exactly what might happen next. He went himself to Washington to cover Congress.

Meanwhile, the *Tribune* pushed on in its progressive rush.
Dana hired a man named Karl Marx to send dispatches from

Europe. Poems that looked like prose but had a great, singing beauty started to appear in the paper. They were signed Walter Whitman. These two new contributors were enough to make conservative people shy away. But this was far from all. The *Tribune* went on an editorial rampage, lashing out at everything from "Demon Rum" to the withholding of equal rights for women. It crusaded for cooperative production among bakers and shoemakers to make "work its own master." It urged— and won—a system of public, tax-supported schools in all New York State. And it insisted that the Constitution should be amended to have U. S. Senators elected by the people instead of selected by the state legislatures. Most of all it continued to condemn the expansion of slavery in the West.

Unquestionably, the *Tribune* was not a newspaper for those of conservative views. Greeley saw the world clearly as it was, and he pressed hard for changes he felt should be made. Most of the issues which Greeley was condemned for supporting are now in the law of the land. But in 1851, there was violent opposition to Greeley's progressive ideas. Many Whigs disagreed with him entirely. In 1851 Raymond started a new newspaper in the city, the New York *Times,* to appeal to more conservative readers. It is the only newspaper that has managed to survive against Greeley's.

Because the *Times* was conservative, it gained immediate acceptance among New York merchants. This meant advertising linage and therefore profit. By the time Raymond's new paper was six months old, Greeley knew he was in for a fierce struggle. The *Times,* Greeley roared, looked at both sides of every question so much that it had trouble telling the two sides apart.

Meanwhile, the controversy in the nation's capital heightened. As Greeley's *Tribune* reached newer and greater success, the nation's struggle over slavery was tearing it apart, dividing it into two factions. Party lines were torn down as the Northern and Southern states grouped together for a desperate battle in Congress over which section would dominate the future of the United States.

The debates centered on the question of expanding slavery in the West. But slavery was only the center of the arguments that divided the country. The North and the South were truly different in the 1850's. The Northern states had great manufacturing centers while the Southern states were basically agricultural. The North wanted a high tariff on goods from foreign lands to protect its own manufactured products from competition. This seemed reasonable. On the other hand, the South pointed out that the tariff only served to make prices higher because the Northern manufacturers were protected from competition. It was unfair, insisted the South, to have to pay whatever price the North wished to place on its products. This too seemed reasonable. Both sides had points in their favor. But neither side would yield an inch. The Southern states —and the Northern states—each wanted to rule the country on their own terms.

Since 1820, an act of Congress known as the Missouri Compromise had been a partial solution to the problems of the groups. At that time, Maine and Missouri were admitted to the Union as "free" state and "slave" state respectively. Most of the southern border of Missouri was on the line of latitude $36° 30'$, and the North and the South agreed that any new states admitted to the Union after Missouri and Maine would be "free" states if they were above this line.

As the new territories in the West were being settled, however, the North and the South began to quarrel once more —this time over new territory and new votes in Congress. Each side wanted the new senators and representatives in order to maintain the balance, and if possible to control the government of the United States itself. After gold was discovered in California in 1848, more than 80,000 "49ers" had gone there the following year to make their fortunes. Congress began debating whether California would be "slave" or "free." While the lawmakers were busy discussing the matter, the Californians were busy making a government that did not include slavery. Tempers flared high as the news reached the Southern group in the capital. It appeared that the United States itself was on the edge of disaster.

Greeley packed his bag quickly and left for Washington. He reported personally for his readers the important Congressional debates and decisions. It was an impressive sight—the great leaders of the Union gathered in the Senate chamber trying to solve the biggest problem the country had yet faced. When Greeley arrived, the California problem was further complicated by the new state of Texas, which was vigorously trying to grab off 125,000 square miles of territory in New Mexico as its own. Texas was a "slave" state; the North was deeply worried because they were counting on New Mexico coming into the Union as a "free" state.

The times called for action and solid leadership. The nation grew nervous waiting for guidance from President Taylor. Nothing came from him but silence. Greeley wrote to his friend, Schuyler Colfax, that Taylor did not "know himself from a side of sole-leather in the way of statesmanship." It was plain to see that if the problem was going to be solved at all, Congress would have to do it. And of all the men in Congress, only one might be able to do it well—the same man who had helped settle the problem in 1820—the "Great Pacificator," Henry Clay. "Perhaps the tallest man in the room," Greeley wrote, Clay "stood upon the floor calm and serene."

Clay's plan had been thought out carefully to appeal to both the North and the South. His speech was just as carefully written. When he rose on the Senate floor, the entire room— its gallery crowded with spectators—was silent. The tall man who had saved the nation once before looked around him, at his friends and at his enemies. Somehow he must bring them together.

"Never so oppressed, never so appalled, never so anxious," Clay's voice rang through the huge Senate room, "I pray God to avert disaster." He paused, his hands gripping the sides of his desk as he spoke. "It is passion, passion and party, that I dread . . . . Let us think only of our God, our country, our conscience and our glorious Union. If any state should choose to place itself . . . against the Union," Clay said, he was for finding out immediately "whether we have a government or not. Even if my own state of Kentucky should attempt it, I would not go with her."

Clay delivered his stirring and patriotic speech with all the drama and power of the master statesman he was. The plan he presented for a compromise was simple: Admit California as a "free" state; organize the territories without reference to slavery; pay Texas $10,000,000 for her claims in New Mexico; and prohibit further slave-trading in the District of Columbia.

These were the basic features of the Compromise of 1850.

The Compromise won a mixed response. Some of the stronger, die-hard Southerners such as John C. Calhoun of South Carolina said it was completely inadequate. Northerners, such as Greeley's old political partner, Seward of New York, found it equally unacceptable. Seward's famous "higher law" speech attacked Clay's proposal. "The Constitution," said Seward, "devoted the domain to Union, to justice . . . and to liberty, but there is a higher law than the Constitution . . ."

The debate went on and Greeley reported it. A committee was formed, with Clay as its chairman, and discussion continued. There was still disagreement, but at least Clay had given Congress something positive to discuss. After more than seven months of debate, the Senate finally accepted Clay's Compromise of 1850. Meanwhile, Taylor had died in office and had been succeeded by Millard Fillmore on July 10, 1850. The Compromise of 1850 was passed by Congress and President Fillmore put his signature on it to make it law. For the last time Congress was successful in preventing a Civil War. When the next crisis came, Clay was dead.

The Compromise of 1850 turned out to be a great victory for the North. With California admitted to the Union a "free" state, the South lost control of both the House and the Senate. The reason was simple, but the South did not notice it until it was too late. The cotton-growing, agricultural areas of the South needed slavery, had a use for it. As the West was settled, it became apparent that slavery was not needed to make the West prosper. It was a severe blow to Southern hopes. They had given up valuable votes in Congress and had no hope of gaining them back as new areas were settled in the West.

[*91*]

During the debate Greeley was firmly on the side of the North. He was always opposed to slavery in any form—and he was always in favor of a high tariff. He reported the position of the South accurately and without any indication of his own feelings and desires. But his editorials were another matter. At first, Greeley was inclined to agree with Seward and the other Northerners who opposed the Compromise. As he viewed the situation, however, and saw how close the nation was to complete collapse, he decided Clay's Compromise was the only way to save the Union. He was right.

The danger of a civil war seemed far away as the year 1850 came to a close. Greeley returned to New York. He was tired and it was good to be home once more.

Only one piece of bad news awaited the editor as he finished one of his most successful years. He learned the final chapter in the story of his good friend Margaret Fuller.

The brilliant woman had gone to Europe in search of even greater knowledge. She had translated into English the plays of Goethe, and she had written *Woman in the Nineteenth Century,* a book demanding equal rights for women. In it she had said that it was ridiculous for love to be a woman's "whole existence." But in Rome she found love herself. She was 38 years old and Giovanni Ossoli was many years younger than she.

Love came late for Margaret Fuller and brought both victory and defeat. Ossoli had no money at all, but their love for each other was great. They had a son, but she never mentioned her marriage and her baby to Greeley or to anyone else. With a new baby and her husband still without money, Margaret decided the only thing to do was to return to America where she could perhaps earn enough money to support the family. On the voyage home their ship was wrecked just off Fire Island. Margaret Fuller, her husband and the child were never seen again.

Losing Margaret Fuller's friendship was difficult. Greeley had admired her greatly and had helped her fight for women's rights in the *Tribune*. Their talks at Turtle Bay had been enjoyable, and even Mary Greeley was in better health when their friend Margaret was with them. Margaret herself explained their friendship best of all when she wrote: "I like, nay more, I love Horace Greeley. He is in . . . his heart a noble man. His abilities in his own way are great. He believes in mine to a surpassing extent."

It was a friendship the great editor could never forget.

Chapter 11

The Tribune Expands

Horace Greeley went back to running the *Tribune*, but Dana and everyone of the staff could see that he was almost completely worn out. He continued to come in around noon and work until almost midnight, writing and editing his paper. For the first time, however, Greeley was in bad humor; his temper would rise quickly over things he would normally shrug off. The preparation of a daily newspaper is a series of battles that must be fought and always—somehow—won.

It is the same now as it was in Greeley's time. Stories are written by reporters. Some are too short, others too long. All must be made to fit into the giant jigsaw puzzle of the page. Advertisements come in late and merchants change their prices—sometimes even the products they are advertising. Big news stories break, and the whole newspaper, or at least a good part of it, must be rearranged to take care of the added material. These things do not happen just once in a while. They

Greeley often worked late at his big, littered desk.

happen every day. When the editor goes to bed, he knows the same thing will face him tomorrow. There will be another paper to get out: empty, white pages to be filled, magically and miraculously arranged to fit, to be ready for the printing press at exactly the right time.

Such had been Horace Greeley's daily battle for ten long years. At last, his energy was gone and he needed a vacation. Frequently, Dana and the other staff members would walk into the editor's office and find him asleep at his desk, his pen still in his hand and an unfinished editorial before him. Dana talked with him, and at last Greeley realized that he needed to get away—at least for a little while. He decided to make a trip to Europe.

Three thousand miles of ocean was a long way for Greeley to put between himself and his newspaper. But he had always wanted to see and know Europe, and this seemed to be the best time for him to go. He packed only one suitcase and left New York on the steamer *Baltic* in April, 1851. Aboard ship, he made "an unloving acquaintance" with the high seas. The *Baltic* plowed through the waters of the Atlantic while Greeley suffered from sea-sickness. He was happy and relieved when the *Baltic* finally docked in England.

Greeley had planned to report the World's Fair in London. He found, however, that he also had been made a judge of exhibits. Then he was asked to make several speeches and even to testify before Parliament on newspaper taxation. Greeley had not counted on any of these added activities. They kept him in England much longer than he had planned.

He left England on June 7 and toured Europe for two months. Everywhere Greeley was the "proud Yankee." He was impressed by the great museums, cathedrals, and many points of interest; but he found each country lacking when compared with his native land. With great joy the Man in the White Coat set sail for home on August 6. He was rested now and eager to get back to his beloved *Tribune*.

"I am glad to find myself back home," he wrote Seward from his old, familiar desk. He remarked that "ruins and antiquities" are nice enough, taken in small doses. But as a general rule, Greeley continued, he preferred a daily newspaper at the breakfast table in his home.

While Greeley was away, the *Tribune* was ably run by Dana. He kept the paper going exactly as its editor would have. Dana worked long hours just as Greeley had always done, and he learned that the full responsibility of publishing the *Tribune* was far greater than being only its managing editor. "It must be better than when the 'Old Man' is at home," he wrote to James S. Pike in Washington, 'or they'll say that Dana's a failure . . . ." Perhaps Dana did not really make the *Tribune* a better newspaper; but when Greeley returned and read the issues he had missed, he found that Dana had done a wonderful job of keeping the *Tribune* on top.

Greeley took over immediately with all his old enthusiasm. His huge desk was piled higher than ever with clippings, copies of other newspapers, and the *Congressional Globes,* which detailed the doings of Congress. There were letters and books and countless small scraps of paper with notes scrawled on them in the editor's almost unreadable handwriting. Greeley seldom cleared and cleaned his desk. It was always cluttered with a thousand different objects, but he always knew where each thing could be found. Even when he was far away in

Europe, no one dared disturb a single sheet of paper. Only a few things were always in the same place: his paste-pot and a box of sand to sprinkle over freshly written editorials for drying the ink. Just above his head, a large pair of scissors hung on a pulley from the ceiling. Another cord, to the side, rang the bell which sent a copyboy hurrying to the busy editor's desk to pick up another editorial. The bell rang loud and often in the first few months after his return.

To partner McElrath, Greeley's bell must have sounded like doom itself, for the editor quickly cost the paper money in a controversy over teaching religion in the public schools of New York. Greeley insisted that public schools should not teach religion at all, that to do so violated the principle of separation of church and state established in the Constitution. At least 2,000 *Tribune* subscribers disagreed by cancelling their subscriptions. Unbothered, Greeley thundered on until the issue was won.

Meanwhile, another political battle was shaping up. Early in 1852, the Whigs were trying to reorganize themselves for another Presidential campaign. For the past three years, Greeley's interest in politics had sunk rather low. He had been keenly disappointed when the Whigs turned to Taylor in 1848, and he had no reason to feel any more encouraged now. Deep inside, Greeley knew the Whig party was dying. As far back as 1847, he had written that he thought "the best party ever yet seen in our country" would come into being. At that time he thought it might be organized in 1852. He was wrong. The Whigs somehow hung together through Taylor's and Fillmore's administrations.

Horace Greeley did not even go to the Whig convention at

Baltimore in June. Only three men stood any chance of winning the nomination—President Fillmore; the great Senator who was one of the Whig founders, Daniel Webster; and another military hero, General Winfield Scott. Of these, Greeley's choice was Scott.

It was not that Horace Greeley liked Scott, for he did not. If anything Greeley liked Scott even less than he had Taylor four years before. Still, he gave Scott the *Tribune's* wholehearted support, even before the nomination. He thought Fillmore and Webster both too conservative and too inclined to favor the South. Scott was the choice of the Whig progressives, who were led by Seward of New York. Seward himself had selected Scott as the best candidate. Among those available, Greeley believed that Scott's ideas were closest to his and that he would be the best man to carry out a progressive government.

There was little question about Scott's winning the nomination. Seward's progressive forces controlled the convention from the beginning. Greeley wrote to Colfax a short while before: "I reckon you see how hopeless things look in the political way. We shall probably run Scott for next President and get flogged at that. I hate it. Win or lose with old 'Fuss and Feathers'—either will be disastrous."

Greeley never hit the truth more squarely. Scott won the nomination with ease. With just as much ease he was defeated by a dark horse Democrat named Franklin Pierce! Scott carried only four states of twenty-eight. The Whigs were hopelessly beaten, never to rise again as a national political party. The *Tribune* faced the issue with honesty, and Greeley wrote: "When a man's head is taken off by a cannon ball, it does not matter whether he has a bullet also in his leg . . . . By Scott's overwhelming defeat the Whig Party is not merely discomfited, it is annihilated."

Not everyone, however, agreed with the *Tribune's* editor. Raymond wrote in the New York *Times* that all the Whigs needed to do was to keep an eye on public affairs, and wait until they were once more wanted by the people. Other Whig newspapers joined in Raymond's optimism about the future of the party. The Troy *Whig* even suggested that if Greeley felt the Whigs were dead, he should get out of the party.

The *Tribune* struck back at its critics sharply. But it must have been mostly out of habit, for its editor considered the Whig party, as such, a dead issue. Greeley entered a new era, one of total political neutrality. Entirely on his own, he began recommending such things as he alone felt were best for the nation.

It was a natural thing to do. No political party at that time reflected all of Greeley's beliefs, or even a large part of them. Ever since the Presidential election of 1844, when Clay lost to Polk, Greeley's devotion to the Whigs had been waning. In 1848, Taylor had been Greeley's last choice. When Taylor died, Fillmore proved to be far too conservative, too inclined toward the South. Then, with Scott, the Whigs were hopelessly divided among themselves: liberals and conservatives in one party. And they suffered a crushing defeat. Greeley had had enough of the Whigs. The Whigs had changed, but Greeley had not.

In the *Tribune,* Greeley continued to campaign for the old familiar issues. On occasion, his editorials raged against the inhumanity of slavery. Often he warned his readers of the

[*101*]

dangers of letting the South expand slavery into the West. Mostly, he concentrated on the actions the nation should consider taking to help make it a better place for all: North or South, rich or poor—regardless of color.

He continued to support equal rights for women, a high tariff to protect the interests of industry from foreign competition, a homestead act for farm laborers in the West, and a cooperative production plan for workers in the cities. Most of all, however, he emphasized the expansion of the United States in the West. In this vast region, Horace Greeley foresaw the huge natural wealth that could someday help make the United States a greater force of democracy and freedom than the world had ever though possible.

"Go west, young man, and grow up with the country," said Horace Greeley—and the nation heard him. If others had used the phrase before, it did not matter; for when the advice came from the thundering *Tribune's* editor it had a new authority.

Greeley backed his famous words with action. He began a vigorous campaign for a railroad to the Pacific Ocean, to link the great West with the large cities of the East. He was so convinced of the value of a Pacific railroad that he was even willing to place it above the question of a high tariff. The entire purpose of the tariff was to protect and advance industry in the North—and to encourage new industries in the South and West. But the tariff was only one way that he felt industry could be helped. He decided that the railroad to the Pacific would be the best way to further the prosperity of the whole country. A Western railroad would increase settlement and would open up new markets for industries in the rest of the nation. With these things in mind, the *Tribune's* editor told opponents of the high tariff that he would make no more mention of that issue if they would join him in his fight for the Pacific railroad.

On the political scene, all seemed quiet. Pike, the *Tribune's* distinguished Washington correspondent, wrote in the *Tribune* of April 30, 1853, a summary of the general feeling of the entire country: "We expect Mr. Pierce will give us a quiet . . . good-for-nothing kind of an Administration, to which nobody will think of making any . . . objection or opposition." Pike even went on to predict that by the end of Pierce's term, there would be a general unity of all parties. It was an enirely inaccurate forecast of the future, but is easy to see how he made the mistake. The Compromise of 1850 seemed to be working well, and the slavery issue appeared to be solved. The country, for a change, seemed united once more. The future looked bright.

In this atmosphere of confidence, Greeley decided the time was right for the *Tribune* to expand. Solon Robinson was named agricultural editor, and the circulation of the *Weekly Tribune*—which appealed to rural families—immediately shot up. George M. Snow was made financial editor, continuing Greeley's policy of hiring experts to head the newspaper's many departments. More than any other publisher, Greeley developed the idea of departments in newspapers, a practice that became a journalistic law.

These additions to the *Tribune's* staff were accepted happily by Greeley's partner, McElrath. But when the editor announced he was going to increase the number of pages in each edition, McElrath and the *Tribune's* advertising manager, Strebeigh, began to complain. The increase in size, along with other improvements Greeley had in mind, would cost $65,000.

The annual expenses of the paper would be greatly increased. Still, Greeley forced his plan into being, and the *Tribune* was enlarged.

Writing to Seward, Greeley explained his hope that a bigger and better *Tribune* would make great gains in circulation. He knew the conservative "cotton Whigs" of New York City did not like the *Tribune* and did not want to spend their advertising money in it. But, he went on in his letter, "it—the cotton Whig element—will advertise with us as freely as it trades with slave drivers—because it will make money by it."

The move proved again Greeley's wisdom. Circulation rose sharply to near 100,000. There were no more complaints from McElrath and Strebeigh as advertising started coming from the conservative merchants. Even with the greatly increased costs of publishing a much larger newspaper, the *Tribune* still showed a net profit of $25,000 for the year. A single share of stock in the paper was worth between $2,500 and $3,000. A bold stroke by Greeley had brought a return on the gamble that was more than he had expected. At last, he was out of debt and the *Tribune* was established as the leading United States daily newspaper, making Greeley's the best known name in the land.

Chapter 12

Drumbeat of the Nation

I n 1853 Horace Greeley moved his family even further into the country. For a while after Pickie died, the Greeleys had lived again in the city. For a New England farm boy, it was not a happy place to be. "Castle Doleful," as he called their home at Turtle Bay, had been unbearable after Pickie was gone. The Greeleys were relieved to move away from so many sad memories. Finally, though, he wanted the country again. He talked it over with Mary and she listed the things she would require in any new country home: "(1) a peerless spring of pure, soft, living water; (2) a cascade or brawling brook; (3) woods largely composed of evergreens."

It was not an easy order. Greeley searched the area around New York and finally found a small farm just east of the village of Chappaqua in Westchester County. It was about 35 miles from downtown New York City, and it filled Mary's requirements. Unfortunately, however, it filled almost none of the requirements of a farm. Located, as Greeley pointed out with some discouragement, on a heavily wooded and very rocky hillside, at the foot of which was a miserable bog, it looked hopeless as a farm. But Horace Greeley had seen wretched land before in his boyhood days, and he determined to work with the place until it was exactly the way he wanted it.

His enthusiasm for his farm at Chappaqua was great. "I should have been a farmer," he wrote. "Its quiet, its segregation from strife, and brawls, and heated rivalries, attract and delight me." He went on to say that he hated having to earn his living in a way that often caused others to suffer, mixing his success as a newspaperman "with others' defeat."

"I should have been a farmer," Greeley said. He might have added—"but I really had no choice." For he had within him the drive and the desire to go to the very top in his profession. When he began his journey with that first job in East Poultney, it was simple. But success makes things more complicated. Soon Greeley's ambition in journalism was as much a part of him as his arms or his legs. It was no longer a matter of his choosing his future. His future had chosen him.

Editing the *Tribune* was much more than a mere job —it was his life. Even though he owned only a fourth of the paper's stock, everyone knew it was Greeley's *Tribune*. He alone made all its decisions, directed the great force of its editorial page, and was the one great reason behind its success. None of Greeley's partners believed the paper could even exist without him.

His responsibility was great, for the *Tribune* had become the leading newspaper in the country. As such, it was up to Greeley to see that, when the *Tribune* printed a story, the facts were right. For when people read things in a newspaper, they believe them. Even more, Greeley was faced with the huge burden of the editorial policy. The *Weekly Tribune* had more than 100,000 readers, and they watched for the editorials signed "H. G." every week. They counted on the *Tribune* to give them the truth. They counted on Greeley's editorials to explain the meaning of it all.

It was one thing for Greeley to sit quietly and tell a friend in Poultney what he thought would be best for the country. It was altogether different with an audience of 100,000, from New York to California, waiting for advice from Greeley— a man most of them had never seen. Greeley knew that when he spoke and wrote he had to be right. He loved the respect that had come to him and to his paper. It was a frightening responsibility.

"Greeley does the thinking for the whole West at two dollars per year for his paper," wrote Ralph Waldo Emerson in the 1850s. Greeley smiled and kept pushing his pen across the paper, recommending what he felt was best for the people.

As with all men whose influence has been great, sometimes the editor of the *Tribune* wished for a simpler life, one with fewer worries and responsibilities. He turned to his farm at Chappaqua in search for the peace he could not find as an editor. He worked with the poor soil on the rocky hillside, getting advice—instead of giving—from his new agricultural editor, Solon Robinson. And soon "Greeley's Bog" at Chappaqua began to take shape as a model farm.

It cost Greeley a small fortune. He never regretted it. He spent over $6,000 on a stone barn, and thousands more on drainage, fertilizing, soil chemistry, subsoil plowing, and the advice of every agriculture expert he could find. Through proper drainage, Greeley used land for planting crops that had never been used before. The bog was cleared out and Mary Greeley's "brawling brook" had water so pure that Horace even kept tin drinking cups along its banks.

"There are many to tell you how much I lose by my farming," Greeley said. "I don't care how much they may laugh at me as an editor or politician, but when they say my farm is a humbug they are a set of blockheads. Have you ever seen better land made from an old bog? All else that I have done may be of no avail, but what I have done here *is* done—it will last."

Without doubt, Horace Greeley's farm at Chappaqua was one of the great joys of his life. Greeley continued to use a small cottage on it for his reading and writing even after a larger house was built on another side of the farm. He loved to go there, for it was quiet and far removed from the heavy burdens of running the *Tribune*.

Only one thing prevented Chappaqua from being the wonderful home that Horace Greeley had hoped for so much— Mary Greeley. Over the years, Horace had done everything he could to make her comfortable and happy. Then, when they moved to Chappaqua and she was still in bed most of the time, complaining about anything and everything she could find, it was obvious that she would never change. Still, they were devoted to each other and Horace was always patient with his wife. Theirs was not a happy marriage in the usual sense. But it was not a failure, either.

Horace was in New York City during the week and was at home only on weekends. Mary made frequent trips out of town and even to Europe, always seeking another doctor to cure her of the many illnesses she thought were hers. It was far from an ideal situation, but they seemed to have an understanding that made it possible to continue their marriage even though there was little joy in it for either of them.

The Greeleys' home at Chappaqua was a happy place for their children, however. Their daughter Gabrielle described Friday evenings there as "the busiest and happiest of the whole week for then father would come home for over Sunday. . . . As a little girl, I would be dressed in my prettiest frock and at train time I would hasten down the lane to meet him." Gabrielle continued, explaining that her father usually brought a "half-dozen bundles of all sizes," filled with gifts for his children and for his wife. "The first place he always sought," she wrote, "was mother's room . . . ."

Those were quiet, happy days for Greeley in 1853. His farm was doing well, the *Tribune* was the mightiest voice in the country, and the nation itself was calmer than it had been for years. There was no way of knowing that the violent controversy over slavery was about to erupt once more, this time to tear the country even further apart than in the dark days before Clay's Compromise of 1850.

Working quietly as the chairman of the Committee on Territories in the Senate of the United States was the Little Giant—Stephen A. Douglas of Illinois. In January of 1854, Douglas announced that his committee had developed a bill to provide for the organization of the territories of Kansas and Nebraska. On the surface, nothing could have sounded duller.

But when Douglas announced the details of his bill, he might as well have hurled a bomb into the Senate chamber.

The Kansas-Nebraska Bill provided for "squatter sovereignty," that the settlers of these territories should decide for themselves whether or not they would have slavery. This was in complete disagreement with the Missouri Compromise of 1820 that allowed slavery only in areas below the southern boundary of Missouri. The passage of such a bill into law would be a clear victory for the South, since it had hoped only to gain control of those areas south of 36° 30'. The North was outraged. The abolitionists, who opposed slavery in any area, even the South itself, were brought to a nearly hysterical anger. When President Pierce announced his approval of the Kansas-Nebraska Bill, the entire North was horrified and the South was overjoyed.

Why Douglas decided to stir the ashes of the slavery question back to a roaring fire is not known. He was interested personally in land speculation and trading in the West, and it was rumored that he wanted to be a candidate for the Democratic Presidential nomination in 1856. Certainly, the passage of the Kansas-Nebraska bill gained him valuable support throughout the Southern states.

Greeley was one of the first to react to Douglas' bill. He had been on a lecture tour as far west as Milwaukee when Douglas introduced his bill. Greeley hurried back and began a series of editorial blasts that were heard throughout the United States. "The passage of the Nebraska Bill," Greeley thundered on January 5, "will arouse and consolidate the most gigantic, determined and overwhelming party for freedom that the world has ever known. We may already see in the future its gathering groups on every hillside, in every valley and on every prairie in the free states."

And again on January 26: "The only question to be answered is whether northern sentiment can be aroused . . . against the atrocious proposition. The fools at Washington believe that it cannot. We believe that it can! *The United States will extinguish slavery before slavery can extinguish the States.*"

More than any other man, Greeley caught the spirit of freedom loving men in the North. *Harper's Weekly* said, "Greeley at once became the banner-bearer of a new party, the herald . . . of a free Union. The daily issue of 'The Tribune' was a startling drum-beat and the 'The Weekly Tribune' became an incessant broadside."

Chapter **13**

War Clouds Gather

The editor of the *Tribune* again went on a lecture tour, this time in Ohio. While there, he took a good sample of public opinion on the Kansas-Nebraska Bill, and he returned even more determined than before to fight it.

Greeley loved the West. He had been urging his fellow citizens to settle the great region as far back as his *New-Yorker* days after the Panic of 1837 had put so many people out of work. Now—in the 1850's—he still saw that the greatness of United States' development lay in the same vast area. He preached its development so much in the *Tribune* that he was known as "Go West Greeley"! But now the West was about to be opened to something that Greeley hated more than anything else: slavery.

For most politicians, Congressmen, and Senators—the question of slavery was only a banner to be carried for identification. The North opposed it; the South was for it. But what really counted was the domination of the United States economy. Both sides wanted to run the country and the Kansas-Nebraska Bill—with slavery as the chief point of difference between the two sides—was the beginning of the battle.

For the South's part, it was unfortunate that some other issue than slavery could not have been found. Defending the slavery of human beings was—and is—impossible. There was no moral excuse for keeping and owning human lives as if they were just another valuable piece of property. It is true that slaveholding practices were not so terrible as Northern writers said they were. Mostly, slaves in the South were treated with kindness by their masters. By the thousands, slaves stood by their masters during the awful years of the Civil War instead of leaving to form a small army of their own to help fight their masters, as the North expected. A few slaves, of course, left, but most of them remained in their homes and lived the way they had always known.

Slaveholding had been practiced for many years, and the Southerners were used to it as just another part of life. The South was unable to understand that there was anything wrong with a system that was working well, and they resented any interference from the North.

But the North did interfere. Here was a weak spot in the Southern claims to power. Here was something that could be attacked with far more fury than the South's preference for a low tariff. The Southerners in Congress fought back. They defended slavery for the simple reason that it was a Southern institution. When Douglas presented the Kansas-Nebraska Bill in the Senate, the Southerners saw their own chance to dominate the North. They moved quickly to get a fast and clear-cut

[*114*]

victory in the heightening struggle for domination.

From beginning to end, Greeley and the *Tribune* fought the Douglas bill. Greeley's concern was not with whether the North or the South dominated Congress. His concern was with man and the continuation of the United States as a democracy —a place of freedom for all men. It would be a tragedy to extend slavery into even more areas than it now held—and particularly it would be tragic to extend it into the West.

Greeley's *Tribune*—the drumbeat of the nation—pounded day after day against the Kansas-Nebraska Bill as it was debated in the Senate. When some conservative Whigs in New York criticized his strong words, Greeley answered them—and at the same time blasted again at Douglas' bill. "We are charged," wrote the editor, "with using harsh and uncharitable language in reference to that scheme [the Kansas-Nebraska Bill]. . . . Our answer to the charge is, that no other language than that we use would faithfully express our sentiments or do justice to our convictions. Were it simply a bad measure, we might speak of it calmly . . . ." But, Greeley said in closing his editorial, the fire of war that Douglas' bill "threatens is not to be extinguished by jets of rosewater." History proved him right.

Meanwhile, the Senate debates went on through the first of March. Finally, after an all-night session, the bill was passed on March 4, 1854, and was sent to the House of Representatives, where it was passed on May 22 and sent to the President's desk. Pierce signed it into law, opening the entire Kansas and Nebraska Territories to slavery and the control of the Southern states.

Greeley and the *Tribune* reacted immediately. "Be It Remembered" blazed across the front page. Beneath it, in a black-bordered box usually reserved for obituaries were the names of each senator and congressman who had voted for the bill. For those who fought it, Greeley wrote: "The gratitude of un-born millions is justly due . . . for on their side are the instincts of Humanity, the spirit of our Age, the hopes of Man and the Justice of God."

With the Kansas-Nebraska Bill now law, Northern anti-slavery forces started coming together to fight for their common interest. Douglas' bill did two things: by reopening the contro-versy over slavery it split the North from the South even further. It also gave the many opponents of slavery a new unity. Old Whigs, Old Democrats and Free Soilers came together in their mutual hatred of slavery. Talk of a new political party to include all these began to spread throughout the entire North and West. The people looked to the editor of the *Tribune* for advice on what should be done next.

Greeley moved slowly but surely. Through most of the summer, he urged the election of "anti-Nebraska" men to Congress, but he did not mention a new political party. Still, it was on his mind a great deal, and he discussed it at length with Thurlow Weed and William H. Seward. Weed was not yet ready to give up on the Whigs as a national political party; Seward, as usual, was ready to go along with whatever Weed wanted.

Despite his interest in a new political party, Greeley could not say much about it in the pages of the *Tribune*. A Democrat named Horatio Seymour had won the New York governor's race in 1852, and Greeley did not want to upset the chances of defeating the Democratic nominee. Weed wanted to name a

Whig to run for governor, and Greeley realized the Democrats could not be defeated without Weed's support. So, for the time being, the *Tribune* remained silent about the new party.

Even so, Greeley actively supported new organizations that sprang up throughout the state. When a convention was called in Allegany County to oppose Douglas' bill, Greeley was asked to suggest a name for the group. His reply has never been forgotten: "Call it Republican—no prefix, no suffix, just plain Republican." The name he suggested had appeal—it was a simple name that carried meaning.

In Ohio, Joseph Medill, later editor of the *Chicago Tribune,* also wrote Greeley for advice. "Go ahead," Greeley replied, "with your proposed Republican party . . . . If you can get the name Republican started in the West it will grow in the East." Other groups throughout the West took the name as well. As they did, they pressed Horace Greeley to give them support in the pages of his paper.

It was a touchy situation. In order to defeat the Democratic candidate for governor, Greeley needed to keep unity with Weed. And Weed wanted to continue the Whig party—with its name—as a national political party. On the other hand, the readers of the *Weekly Tribune* in the West were insisting on some form of support from Greeley. Finally, on June 16, 1854, he printed an editorial "Party Names and Public Duty." He explained that he had not taken much interest in the name the opponents to the Kansas-Nebraska Bill used, for he felt the freedom most needed was freedom "from party names and party shackles." He went on to say that he agreed with the policies of both the Whigs and the Free-Soil Democrats—and that he would like to see the two groups united into one party.

"We should not care," he continued, "whether those united were designated Whig, Free Soil Democrats or something else; though we think that some simple name like Republican" would be best.

The editorial satisfied the new Republicans in the West, but it did not please Weed at all. In New York, Greeley's editorial stirred up even more talk of a Republican party, and Greeley was in the thick of the efforts to organize it. Finally a group met in Saratoga, New York, on August 16, to discuss the possibilities of a new party in the state. Enough of Weed's men were there to prevent any definite decisions. Weed did not attend the meeting himself. But he sent Raymond, the editor of the New York *Times,* to see to it that the meeting did not succeed in creating a new party. The group decided to meet later in the year at Auburn.

At the second meeting, in September, the Whigs nominated Myron Clark for governor—and Raymond of the *Times* for lieutenant-governor. For the "partner" in the well-known political firm of Weed, Seward, and Greeley, this was an open slap in the face. Before the convention, Greeley realized that Raymond was rising in favor with Weed. The *Times* was often getting stories from Albany that the *Tribune* did not receive. It was plain that Weed was shifting from Greeley to Raymond as the voice of the Whig party in New York City.

Weed's actions hurt Greeley very much. He continued to support the Whig candidates, however, until after the election. The Whigs won by a slim majority of 309 votes. Without the support of the *Tribune,* there is no doubt that they would have lost. The editor had promised his support, and he kept his word.

With the election over, however, Greeley attacked. In a blistering editorial, the *Tribune* criticized Seward for not having supported the organization of the new Republican Party in New York. Greeley said Seward "stood aside" and allowed the movement to go forward without "a word of bold and hearty encouragement or sympathy." Two days later, Greeley struck again at Seward and Weed. He feared the time for organizing the Republican Party in New York was past—and that Seward was to blame for not having led the way. On the same day, November 11, 1854, Greeley wrote a letter to Seward. In it, he resigned from Weed, Seward, and Greeley, the political firm that had been running Whig affairs in New York State for 14 years.

Point by point, Greeley listed his complaints. He reminded Seward that after his election as governor of the state, with much help from Greeley, absolutely nothing was done to help the editor in his struggle to get out of debt. It did not occur to him, Greeley wrote, that Seward could have helped, but "I now think it should have occurred to *you*. . . . I was not the man to ask you for it; I think that should not have been necessary." He also mentioned how much it had hurt him to see his rival, Raymond of the *Times*, receive the Whig nomination for lieutenant governor. In closing Greeley said he hoped he would never be in opposition to Seward's running for a public office. He even promised to support him the following February for re-election to the Senate of the United States. Greeley warned, however, "thereafter I may take such course as seems best, without reference to the past."

Seward found it difficult to believe that the "partner" was really resigning. He took Greeley's letter as being only the result of a temporary anger that would soon be forgotten. In reply, Seward urged the "partner" to let "bygones be bygones."

Greeley wrote a final letter to Seward on November 24. In it he explained that he did not wish to "reopen the past." By this time, some of Greeley's first anger was gone. Weed and Seward felt sure that in a short while everything would be the same as it had been for 14 years.

It was a bad mistake, for Horace Greeley meant every word he had said.

Within a month, Greeley's attention was turned away from New York state politics. He concentrated on the further organization of the Republican Party and his battle against slavery. In December of 1854 Horace Greeley announced that he no longer would be satisfied with a return to the Missouri Compromise, which allowed slavery in any area below 36° 30′. In passing the Kansas-Nebraska Bill, allowing slavery in territories above the line, the South had destroyed the meaning of the Missouri Compromise. Greeley felt the South was trying to extend slavery throughout the entire United States. The position of the North, Greeley said, should now be to eliminate slavery entirely from all areas of the country.

For the first time since the Kansas-Nebraska Bill became law, the North was beginning to move to the attack. The attack —quite naturally—was led by Horace Greeley.

The year 1854 came to a close. The battle against slavery was getting hotter. As "the drumbeat of the nation," his own *Tribune* led all the way. Toward the end of January, 1855, Greeley kept his earlier promise to help re-elect Seward to the U. S. Senate. Senators were still chosen by the state legislatures, rather than by popular vote as they are today. So, Greeley went to Albany and helped his old partner into the Senate once more. With that job done, he returned to New York City and his newspaper.

But he was tired and felt little interest in another long year of hard work. His farm at Chappaqua did not help much, for Mary and the children had been in Europe since the fall of 1854. Chappaqua was not the same without his family. Still, he worked on through the winter, sometimes spending the weekends in his empty house at Chappaqua, but often staying in New York until time to go to work again on Monday morning. It was an unhappy and lonely way to live, and once more Dana noticed it.

Early in the spring, Dana began urging Greeley to take another trip to Europe. He could join his family and have a good vacation. Finally, in April, the editor agreed. Once again he packed his single suitcase, and tossed his famous white coat over his shoulder. He was ready to renew his "unloving acquaintance with the sea."

When he arrived in England he went straight to London to meet his wife and children. This time, however, he did not remain in England very long. A world's fair was being held in Paris, and Greeley wanted to see it. He gathered his family together and they left immediately for France. There, Greeley, the most famous editor in the United States of America, was promptly tossed in jail!

Greeley had been one of the stockholders in the Crystal Palace Exposition in New York City in 1851. Many valuable pieces of art—paintings and sculpture—were damaged. What Horace Greeley did not know was that, under French law, all

The French police swarmed about Greeley as he got down.

of the stockholders were responsible for losses at the exposition. A French sculptor, Auguste Lechesne knew Greeley was in Paris, and he demanded $2,500 in gold for a statue of his that had been ruined during the New York showing.

Greeley was amazed to discover that under French law he could be held responsible for Lechesne's loss. He was brought before a French judge and told to appear in court the following week. A little later, Greeley was stopped on the street by several French policemen who did not understand

[*122*]

English. Greeley, in turn, could not speak French. As they all tried to talk, the situation became more and more confused. At last, Greeley started to get out of his carriage. The policemen, who thought the judge had not really released Greeley, decided he was trying to escape. Quickly, they grabbed Greeley and pushed him back into the carriage. By now everyone was shouting. In the confusion, the policemen decided the only thing to do was to carry him off to jail. With both sides still shouting—and still not understanding a single word—they drove away to Clichy prison.

Greeley was there from Saturday afternoon until late Monday afternoon. During his stay everyone who was an acquaintance of his in Europe came to see the great editor in jail. Of course, Mary came on the very first day bringing her husband a fine-tooth comb and his nightshirt! There were many other visitors who came only out of curiosity. But these, Greeley wrote later in a humorous description of his jail term, were not allowed to bother him. He also complimented the prison on its democratic methods in treating all prisoners equally well, with no special favors for anyone.

When he was released, Greeley quickly took his family to Switzerland. They rented a small cottage at Lausanne, where they remained through the rest of June and part of July. But the lawsuit over Lechesne's statue was still unsettled, and Greeley had to go back to Paris late in the month. Shortly thereafter, he decided he had had enough of Europe; so he quietly went back to England and took the next ship for home.

Chapter 14

Greeley Goes West

Horace Greeley returned to New York City in August of 1855, ready to jump once more into the "boiling sea of politics." The *Tribune* had been run well, under Dana and Pike. Circulation was now close to 180,000 copies for all editions, and advertising profits continued to rise.

In politics as well, Greeley was greeted by good news. A Republican state committee had been formed and a convention was to meet in Syracuse on August 24. Thurlow Weed, seeing that the Whig party was truly dead, had come over to the Republican side and was quickly taking charge of the new party in the state. Seward, as expected, followed Weed's lead. "It is the party for us!" he said happily. Only a few months earlier he had ignored Greeley's urgent request to come out in favor of the new party in the state.

After the fall elections, the anti-slavery forces appeared to have a small majority in the House of Representatives at Washington. There was even a chance that a Republican could be elected Speaker of the House. Sensing this opportunity and knowing that a bitter struggle could come in Congress over it, Greeley decided to go himself to report the proceedings to the readers of the *Tribune*.

He arrived in Washington in time for the first meeting of the House on December 3. He sent his report back to New York: "For the first time in history the House has a majority made up of anti-slavery members . . . ." The opportunity was there, and the Republicans began working hard to elect their first Speaker. Nathaniel P. Brooks of Massachusetts was the Republican choice, and Greeley supported him all the way.

Trying to get Brooks named Speaker was a hard struggle, for the South was well organized and ready to fight. Debates dragged on. Greeley was quickly making enemies among the Southern politicians in the capital. Near Christmas he wrote to Dana in New York: "It does me good to see how those who hate 'The Tribune' much, fear it more."

Greeley became one of the best known men in Washington. The House was still unable to elect a Speaker, and tempers on both sides grew shorter every day. Among Republicans and other anti-slavery Congressmen, Greeley became immensely popular. The Southern Democrats were developing a tremendous hatred for the Man in the White Coat. One by one, Greeley ripped into those who opposed Brooks as speaker. One of these was a congressman from Arkansas, Albert J. Rust.

Greeley blasted in the *Tribune* at Rust late in January of 1856. It was the usual Greeley editorial—full of hard, biting words that ate deep into the pride of Congressman Rust. He was not a man to take Greeley's bitter words lying down. Rust decided something had to be done to even the score with Greeley.

At first Rust thought of challenging the editor to a duel. But he learned that Greeley's opinion of dueling was rather low. Still, it was the preferred way for Rust. He waited a few days, trying to decide what to do.

Then one day he spotted Greeley on Capitol Hill. The editor was walking quietly along toward Pennsylvania Avenue. Rust began moving toward him rapidly. Greeley saw the man coming, but with his nearsighted eyes he thought it was only a drunken man staggering along. He was shocked as the man angrily stopped before him.

"Would you resent an insult?" Rust demanded. .

"I don't know, sir," the editor said quietly.

Rust scowled at Greeley and asked him if he were a dueling man.

"That depends on circumstances," Greeley replied. An air of superiority in his voice made Rust even angrier. Without warning, the congressman lashed out at the unsuspecting editor and smashed home a hard right to Greeley's jaw!

Shaken badly, Greeley slammed into the fence along the sidewalk. Momentarily, he stood dazed. Rust must have thought his blow would end the fight, for he left at once. It is likely that Rust made a wise decision, for Greeley was a large man, heavily built through the shoulders from his long hours of chopping wood at Chappaqua. Had he struck Rust with the same surprise, it is doubtful that the Arkansas Congressman would have stayed on his feet. Greeley shook his head a couple of times and looked around for his opponent.

By this time, Rust was hurrying along. Greeley, however,

[*127*]

was far from satisfied that this was the end of the fight. He moved quickly down the street, determined to even the score. After several blocks he found Rust in front of the National Hotel. Rust seemed to want no part of another exchange. But Greeley's Yankee temper was up, and he began telling Rust exactly what he thought of him. At last, Rust had heard enough. He threatened Greeley again with a duel. In detail, Rust described what he would do if the editor would only meet him.

"I don't shelter myself under that plea," said Greeley slowly. Rust could not mistake his meaning: that Rust was afraid to stand up and fight.

The editor was right. Rust did not throw another punch. He had already seen Greeley shrug off the best he could offer without even falling. Rust was carrying a heavy cane in his hand. As suddenly as he could, he spun it through the air in a wide arc and aimed it at Greeley's head. This time the editor was ready.

The heavy cane sailed toward him with tremendous and deadly force. Just as it was almost to him, Greeley put up his left arm and caught the full force of the blow. As Rust's weapon fell useless to the ground, Greeley grabbed the Congressman's shirt. Fortunately for Rust, that was all there was to it. A crowd came between the two and pulled Greeley back from Rust.

Although a full-fledged fight never developed, Greeley proved that his courage was not limited to what he wrote. He was ready to back up his words with action. The surprising thing, really, is that this was the first time in all the years Greeley had been an editor that someone had physically attacked him. The nineteenth century was a rowdy time. Almost every newspaper editor was called on at one time or another to back up his words with his fists. For some reason, Greeley was not bothered in this way. He was a large man, impressive in his famed white coat and heavy boots. For whatever reason, the *Tribune's* editor was left pretty much alone by those who would have attacked other editors of the time.

A few days after the encounter with Rust, the Republicans succeeded in winning the Speaker's chair for Brooks. It appeared for a few days that Greeley might be able to return to New York. Other struggles in the Congress followed quickly, however, as the North and the South continued their fight. Unhappily, Greeley decided to remain in Washington and report the activity for his readers. He continued to set the course for his newspaper's editorial pages, even though he was many miles from New York City.

On one occasion, Dana approached Greeley about publishing a Sunday "picture newspaper." Dana obviously was getting ideas of his own while the boss was out of town. Greeley snuffed out the idea quickly. He wrote to Dana: "I look suspiciously on that magazine project because I regard 'The Tribune' as a great idea just begun to be developed. . . . Better do one thing well than several middling well. To make 'The Tribune' the first newspaper in America is fortune and fame enough for us, and we are doing that now. Let us try to do what we have undertaken before we apply our energies to printing picture books."

In addition to pushing the *Tribune* to the top, Greeley was also working as hard as he could to organize the Republicans as a truly national political party. When a convention was held at Pittsburgh in February of 1856, Greeley attended. He was greatly pleased to see delegations from eight of the "slave" states. He wrote in the *Tribune* that the Pittsburgh convention represented a truly "national party, based upon the principle of Freedom." Greeley firmly believed that the Republican party could gain strength quickly, even in the South. He believed in the basic wisdom of mankind, and he felt sure many thousands of people throughout the South would rally to the party's great purpose to eliminate slavery from the United States. He even went so far as to state that the Republican party would become "a strong if not the strongest party in every State."

This confidence of Greeley's shows clearly that he never desired to create the conflict between the North and the South. He always felt that all the United States should be brought together in a mutual goal of freedom and democracy. He would never have become a leader of the Republican party if he had not been sure it was in the best interests of the entire nation. The "slave" states, Greeley felt certain, were only waiting for the clear call of the Republican party to show them the way to wisdom, justice, and freedom for all.

In this spirit of a great crusade for the freedom of every American, Horace Greeley went to the national convention in 1856 to help select a candidate for the Presidency. For a change, Greeley and Weed were in agreement on the best candidate, John Charles Fremont—the "Pathfinder of the West," —a young soldier and explorer with great popular appeal. With the support of the *Tribune* and Weed's powerful political machine, Fremont won the nomination as the Republican's first Presidential candidate.

The Republican platform showed the strong influence of Greeley. He wrote much of it personally, and the strong Greeley style was easy to spot. The platform included nearly all of Greeley's political sentiments: opposition to slavery, the building of a Pacific railroad, and free soil in the West. Enthusiasm for the new party and its glamorous candidate ran high at the convention. It was reflected in the Republican's bouncy campaign song:

> Then let the shout again
> Ring out from sea to sea,
> Free Speech, Free Press, Free Soil, Free Men,
> Fre—mont and Victory.

It was a grand beginning, and Greeley left the convention with great hopes of victory. He returned to the *Tribune* office and began writing editorials to help the Fremont cause.

Meanwhile, the Democratic party nominated a well known political figure, James Buchanan of Pennsylvania. Buchanan had been out of the country as the minister to England and therefore had had no connection with the Kansas-Nebraska controversy. He ran on a platform that supported the Kansas-Nebraska Act. What was left of the old Whig party— and the Know Nothings—nominated former President Millard Fillmore on a platform which evaded the slavery question altogether. Fillmore got just enough votes in the election to split the Republican forces. Buchanan, the Democrat, won.

Still, the results were encouraging to the new Republican party. More than 1,000,000 votes had been cast for Fremont and, as Greeley said, the party had "a grand future before it". During the months that followed Buchanan's election, Greeley kept working to make the Republican party stronger. He brought in many of the old Whigs and "Know Nothings"— even old Democrats who were unhappy with President Buchanan's support of the Kansas-Nebraska Act. Anyone, in Greeley's mind, who opposed slavery and favored freedom throughout America should be in the Republican party. Time after time, he urged citizens to come over to the new party, and his words reached a larger audience than ever before. During the heat of the Presidential campaign, the circulation of the *Tribune,* including the weekly edition which was widely read in the West, had jumped to about 280,000 copies. Even after the election when circulation fell off, the *Tribune* was being read by more than 230,000 families. In every sense, it was the voice of the Republican party.

Late in the year, two important things happened. First, Greeley came to friendly terms with the author of the Kansas-Nebraska Act, Senator Douglas! And second, growing out of the first, Greeley had his first contact as a journalist with Abraham Lincoln.

A little earlier the Kansas legislature had met and forced through a constitution which made slavery legal. Without submitting the constitution to the people, they sent it to Washington. Kansas had been settled mostly by people who opposed slavery. If the Lecompton Constitution, as it was called, had been put to a vote in Kansas, it would not have passed. Clearly, this was politics at its worst. Matters were made even worse when President Buchanan stated in a message to Congress in December of 1857 that he favored admitting Kansas to the Union under the Lecompton Constitution.

Immediately, Douglas was furious. His Kansas-Nebraska Act had been designed to allow the people in new areas to decide for themselves. The Lecompton Constitution was thus clearly a fraud. Douglas even carried his argument to the White

House in an interview with President Buchanan. They argued violently and Buchanan threatened to ruin Douglas' political career. Angered even more, Douglas reminded the President that the days of President Jackson's strong-armed administration policies were long gone. The two men parted on poor terms and a terrible split was created in the Democratic party.

Most Republicans viewed this new division of the Democrats with joy. Greeley, of course, was among them. He and others began to applaud Douglas' stand for an open election in the Kansas Territory, since it would mean victory for the free states of the North. Suddenly, Douglas was no longer hated by the Republicans. Greeley even saw a way to use the Democratic senator to further the Republican cause.

Greeley saw that if Douglas were re-elected to the Senate of the U. S., he would continue to cause the Democrats—especially the Southern Democrats—a great deal of grief. Eventually, they might even kick him out of the party. Meanwhile, he could be the most effective weapon available against those who were trying to extend slavery in the West. Editorials appeared in the *Tribune,* actually urging Republicans in the Illinois legislature to back, of all people, Stephen A. Douglas!

Other Republican newspapers, joined the *Tribune* in fighting for Douglas' return to the Senate. Raymond's New York *Times* and the Springfield, Mass., *Republican* both supported the Little Giant of Illinois. Shortly, however, a strong voice from Illinois told the Eastern newspapers to keep out of Illinois politics. The Chicago *Tribune* reminded the Eastern editors that politics in Illinois was the concern of only the people of Illinois. Further, it pointed out that the Republicans had a promising candidate for the Senate—and that it was

Greeley's duty to support him. His name was Abraham Lincoln.

"What does 'The Tribune' mean," wrote Lincoln, "by its constant . . . admiring and magnifying of Douglas? . . . if 'The Tribune' continues to din his praises into the ears of its five or ten thousand subscribers in Illinois, it is more than can be hoped for that all will stand firm."

William H. Herndon, a law partner of Lincoln and a firm Republican supporter, even made a trip East to win support away from Douglas and for Lincoln. Shortly after Herndon's visit with Greeley, the *Tribune* declared that because of the Lincoln-Douglas debates "Lincoln has decidedly the advantage." Until the election, the *Tribune* was in the corner of the Republican Rail-Splitter. It was already August of 1858, however, and Douglas had gathered enough votes in the legislature to re-elect the Little Giant over Lincoln.

During the next several months, Greeley concentrated on his newspaper without much thought of politics. The year 1857 had brought a financial panic. The *Tribune's* advertising volume was hit fairly hard; circulation that had dropped after the Presidential election in 1856 was slow to pick up again. To make matters worse, Greeley's long-time partner, Thomas McElrath, went bankrupt and was forced to sell his *Tribune* stock and retire from the paper. Horace Greeley tried to help, but McElrath's financial troubles were more than could be remedied by Greeley, who seldom had an extra penny to his name. With McElrath gone, the editor was forced again to be the business manager of the *Tribune* as well. This time, his record was somewhat better. By the start of 1859, circulation was back to 210,000 from a low of 190,000. Advertising returned to

After a long train ride, Greeley reached his beloved West.

normal as the *Tribune* once more had an upswing in circulation. In April the *Tribune* was reaching 211,750 families, and its
editor felt confident enough to begin making plans for a trip
he had wanted to take for a long time. On May 9, he boarded
a train and began the great journey through the West he loved
—all the way to California.

For Greeley, it was a great trip. It was also a hard one.
The trains moved slowly and, as Greeley described them for
his loyal readers, they reached new heights of discomfort. The
sleeping car was filled with stale, sickening air and the drinking
water had a horrible taste. He suffered the discomforts of the
train all the way to St. Joseph, Missouri. There he took a barge
down the Missouri River to Atchison, Kansas. "I have long
been looking for the Far West and here it is!" he said with
obvious joy.

From Atchison he kept going by stagecoach over the Kansas plains into the great Rockies and on to Denver. He wrote of the trip: "I haven't slept in a bed in a month, nor with any floor under me but Mother Earth, traveling among Indians, buffaloes, wolves, antelope and a few white men. Yet I like Kansas." Here was a true Westerner!

In all, Greeley loved the West, and the West loved Greeley. The people sensed that he was really one of them, even if he was a New England Yankee. Everywhere he went he urged the Westerners to continue their fight to get a railroad built to the Pacific Ocean, to develop their land, their cities and industries. All this, coming from the editor of the New York *Tribune,* made Greeley something of a hero. After he was gone, the legend of his travels in their country began to grow— with many tales of the New York editor's experiences going around the campfires.

One of the most famous concerned a stagecoach trip Greeley took with a man named Hank Monk as driver. Greeley was in a great hurry to get from Carson City to Placerville for a speaking engagement. The stage was running a little late, so Greeley told Hank Monk to get him there as quickly as possible. He cracked the whip and drove the team at a breakneck pace, shaking the coach so much that it "jolted the buttons all off Greeley's coat and finally shot his head clear through the roof of the stage," as Mark Twain later described it in *Roughing It.* The stage kept going at terrific speed; and Greeley, though shaken up, made his speaking engagement on time.

The legend lived—and the legend grew—and the name of Horace Greeley became one of the best loved in the wonderful country he helped so much to develop.

Chapter 15

Making a President

Horace Greeley returned from his trip to the West in October of 1859, happy and rested. He was ready to return to the heavy duties of the *Tribune* and eager to see a Republican President elected in 1860. New York City itself was a happy town that fall—growing, bustling, and glamorous. No one knew that just beyond the horizon were the dark clouds of a civil war.

Greeley was still trying to catch up with the work that had piled up while he was away when news came that John Brown and a small band of men had raided the United States arsenal at Harper's Ferry, Virginia. Excitement broke out in the *Tribune* office as the telegraph brought in the details of the startling attack. Brown was almost a fanatic in his opposition to slavery. He decided to attack the arsenal, arm the slaves, and lead them to victory and freedom. A dedicated man, he believed he was right, but his action was wrong. United States

Army troops under the command of Colonel Robert E. Lee and Lieutenant J. E. B. Stuart captured Brown's group with ease, and six weeks later John Brown was hanged for treason against the government of the United States.

With John Brown's raid, the clouds of war were no longer beyond the horizon. Darkly they appeared like an approaching storm. Even though the people in the North realized John Brown's raid was a bad thing, the South was horrified and furious in its anger. As 1859 ended and the election year of 1860 began, there was an even more serious split than had ever before been known.

Such was the spirit of the nation as it entered the Presidential election year. Among the Democrats, Douglas was the strongest man. He had a great deal of opposition in the South, however, because he insisted the territories in the West should "decide for themselves" on slavery. Douglas became the Presidential candidate of the northern Democrats, but John Breckenridge of Kentucky ran as the southern Democratic nominee. Breckenridge, naturally, favored full protection for slavery. Still another group, the Constitutional Unionists, nominated John Bell of Tennessee on a platform that sought to solve the slavery problem by ignoring it completely.

So three candidates for the Presidency would oppose the Republican candidate. It looked certain at first that the Republicans would nominate William H. Seward of New York, who, of course, had the backing of Thurlow Weed's powerful political machine. It had controlled many Whig party conventions in the past—and even the first Republican convention, which nominated Fremont. Seemingly, whoever Weed wanted nominated, usually was nominated.

[*138*]

This year, however, there were many who were unwilling to accept Weed's candidate without a fight. The strongest contender was Abraham Lincoln. Another candidate, Edward Bates of Missouri, had powerful support.

Greeley was not named as a New York delegate and attended the convention in Chicago as a delegate of the new state of Oregon. He was convinced that now—with the nation in such a serious situation—it would be a mistake to nominate Seward. Greeley did not feel that Seward was a bad man, only that he was controlled too much by the political boss, Weed. So, searching elsewhere for a man who could meet the dangerous days ahead, Greeley turned to Bates of Missouri. Bates had been a slaveholder, but had freed all his slaves. He was an admirer of Clay and was generally in agreement with Greeley. He was a quiet, dignified man, the sort who could be trusted in a crisis.

As for the Rail-Splitter of Illinois, Greeley was not certain. "Lincoln has a host of friends out here who see in him something that the rest of us have not yet seen." Greeley admitted there must be "something" about the Rail-Splitter that was very good indeed, or he would not have convinced so many people that he could save the nation from destruction. The one thing Greeley was sure of as the convention started was that Seward should not be the Republican candidate.

On May 16, Greeley sent a telegram to the *Tribune*, saying that Seward's chances were about even to win the nomination. By the next day, his wire stated that Seward was gaining ground fast and that it appeared he would win when balloting began the next day. But during the night Greeley went to work. He talked with every state delegation he could find in their hotel rooms. Lincoln was the only man who had any chance at all of beating Seward, and Greeley moved to the Rail-Splitter's side in urging everyone to move away from Weed's hand-picked man. Greeley spent a long and desperate night of talking.

Finally, on May 18, the balloting began. Just as expected, Seward led Lincoln on the first ballot by 173½ votes to 102. But it was not enough to win the nomination. On the second ballot, Lincoln picked up ground. Seward had 184½ and Lincoln had 181! The Seward forces were frightened as they saw Greeley moving among the delegates, still talking, still fighting to gain the nomination for Lincoln. When the voting began again, more Seward votes were being switched to the Rail-Splitter. Weed knew that his political machine was about to suffer its worst defeat—and at the hands of Horace Greeley. Before the final votes were even officially announced, Seward had his name withdrawn, thus eliminating all competition to Lincoln.

The entire convention knew exactly what had happened and who was responsible. They crowded around the *Tribune's* editor and cheered him as if he had received the Presidential nomination. His work had been the major force in making Lincoln the nominee of the Republican party. The editor's face burst into a broad grin, for it was a great victory for him personally and he was certain that it was for the best interests of the Republicans and of the country. As he stood among the cheering delegates, it was the happiest time Greeley had ever known.

Weed, of course, was miserable. Not only had his own candidate, Seward, lost the nomination. He had lost it because

On the convention floor, Greeley won over votes for Lincoln.

of a man who once was their "junior partner." As Weed said, Greeley was a man he "had taken out of an attic printing office and made prominent." What Weed forgot was that Greeley had a mind of his own. At the Republic convention, the editor of the *Tribune* had the wisdom to know that a President who—like Seward—would take orders from a political boss was not the man to have in the White House.

In the following weeks Weed launched a bitter attack against Greeley. His new "junior partner"—Raymond of the

Times led the assault, saying Greeley had only sought revenge on Seward. Greeley pointed out that he and Seward had been friends for many years and that "if I had been swayed by feeling alone I should have preferred him to any of his competitors. But I did not, and I do not, believe it advisable that he should be the Republican candidate for President."

Most Republicans agreed with Greeley. An important Republican from Indiana wrote: "Greeley has slaughtered Seward but has saved the Republican Party." The Rail-Splitter had caught the spirit of the party, and Republicans were happy that Greeley had helped nominate the tall, sad-faced man. Even then the Republicans knew that—mostly because of Horace Greeley—a great man stood at the head of their party.

With Lincoln running against three other candidates, Weed joined with Greeley to help elect him. The campaign was not easy, for Lincoln and the Republicans stood for many things that were unpopular, especially in the South. Even though the platform said nothing about ending slavery in the South, it was difficult for Southerners to believe that Lincoln was in any way on their side. All they had to do was remember what he had already said—that the government could not endure "half slave and half free." There was little doubt which side Lincoln would be on if a decision had to be made.

So, the South was given up as hopelessly lost to Breckenridge. The Republicans knew they absolutely must carry the important states of New York, Pennsylvania, New Jersey, Indiana, and Illinois, if they hoped to win. No one worked harder than Greeley and his New York *Tribune*.

Beside daily editorials, Greeley also helped arrange for speakers in the New York area. He printed a campaign pamphlet *Political Textbook for 1860* which he helped to write. He helped raise money to pay campaign expenses. By August, Greeley was speaking at least three times a week. He even wrote a campaign song, "The March of the Free."

As the campaign swung to its climax, Greeley's *Tribune* blasted at Lincoln's opponents daily. And Greeley's newspaper was now the greatest voice in America. Circulation was up to almost 300,000. The *Tribune* was the largest newspaper in the world.

Finally, in early October, the first returns came into the *Tribune* office. Lincoln had swept to victory in Pennsylvania. "Boys, We've Got 'Em" shouted the *Tribune* in a banner head-line. Indiana and Ohio followed with victories for Lincoln. The Republicans felt, for the first time, that victory was in sight. Even so, Greeley and the *Tribune* did not let up. The Republican party was young and had never won a national election. It was no time to be over-confident, and Greeley knew it.

Then, in November, the final results came in. Support for Lincoln in the South was disappointing. Apparently the South felt that Lincoln's promise to allow slavery in their states was not really sincere. Their votes were split among the other three candidates, showing the South's confusion as to who would be their best friend in the White House. This confusion in the South to a large degree won the election for Lincoln. In the North, Lincoln scored a solid victory in 18 states, enough to give the great Rail-Splitter 1,866,000 votes. Fewer than 30,-000 of these came from the Southern states. It was a bitter disappointment to Greeley, who hoped from the start that the Republican party would be truly national. It was a noble hope that Greeley had held—it was a noble ambition of the

[*143*]

Republican party. But in 1860, the election of Lincoln was far from being a national victory. With his victory the clouds of war rose darkly until they overshadowed the entire nation with gloom and fear.

Within a few days the South Carolina legislature called for a state convention to consider secession, withdrawal from the United States of America. The convention met on December 10 and South Carolina declared that she had "resumed her place among the nations of the world." Only six weeks later, South Carolina had been joined by Mississippi, Georgia, Florida, Alabama, Louisiana, and Texas in seceding from the Union.

The North was stunned. Lincoln was not yet in office and already seven states had left the Union. President Buchanan hesitated. He had only a few more months in office. The North was torn between cries of war and cries for peace "at any price." In the *Tribune* Greeley took a calm stand. He warned the nation of the horrors of war and said that the Union should let the Southern states "depart in peace."

It was an unusual thing for Greeley to say, but he had a sound reason. In his view, the United States was one nation, not many small ones. He felt that each part needed all the others. He felt that the South—if it left the Union—would soon come back on its own. He also felt sure that the majority of Southerners would not vote to leave the Union if the question were put before them. He urged a free election in the South to make the decision honestly.

But the forces against Greeley's proposal grew stronger. In early February, 1861, still before Lincoln's inauguration, the Southern states met in Montgomery, Alabama, and formed a new government, the Confederate States of America.

Still, a shot had not been fired. Buchanan did nothing, and the North argued over whether the South could end the Union in this way or not. Some said the Union could not be destroyed. Others said that it could. Meanwhile, the South went its way, setting up its new national government with Jefferson Davis as president.

Weed suggested extending the line of the old Missouri Compromise all the way west to the Pacific—with slavery anywhere below the line. Greeley opposed any further compromise and found that one who agreed with him was the President-elect, Abraham Lincoln. When Lincoln's view was clear, further talk of a compromise ended. The North did nothing. It waited for the new President's term to begin.

In his inaugural address, Lincoln left no doubt. The government of the United States could not be destroyed. He expressed a kind feeling toward the South, but there was no question of his meaning when he promised to "preserve, protect and defend" the Union. He denied that the Southern states had any right under the Constitution to leave the Union. "I am loathe to close," the new President said, "We are not enemies, but friends . . . ." Lincoln's beautiful and powerful speech urged the Southern states to return in peace. Just behind the President sat the editor of the *Tribune*. He had come to Washington to report Lincoln's speech. He listened carefully, his eyes fixed on the back of Lincoln's head, watching this man who was now the President—and who would never have been nominated without the help of the Man in the White Coat.

Greeley heard the great man's voice soar above the crowd,

drifting off into the distant silence of the sunny day. Greeley knew that Lincoln's words—mighty though they were—might never reach so far as the hearts of the rebel leaders.

Chapter 16

The Storm Breaks

T he answer to Lincoln's inaugural address came with a cannon shot fired on Fort Sumter in South Carolina on April 12, 1861. Thus began the Civil War.

After the Southern states had seceded, a problem arose of what to do about the U. S. Army forts in Southern territory. Lincoln decided not to recognize the independence of the Confederacy. He wrote the governor of South Carolina, telling him that supplies were being sent to Fort Sumter. The Confederacy reacted quickly. President Davis ordered General Pierre Beauregard—with a force of about 7,000 men—to demand surrender of the fort to the Confederate army.

Major Robert Anderson, commander of the Union forces at Fort Sumter, had only a hundred men; but he refused to surrender. So the Confederates opened fire. For two days Anderson held out. At last, however, when the fort had been set on fire by heavy artillery, Anderson surrendered. Union supplies had not arrived. The Confederates allowed Anderson and his men to return to the North—with full honor.

The attack on Sumter came too early in the morning for the *Tribune* to carry the story that day. But on April 13, Greeley announced to the nation that "the Jeff Davis rebellion" was now at war with the government of the United States. "Let none doubt the ultimate triumph of the Right."

Greeley had long had the desire to save the nation from a terrible civil war. But he had opposed a compromise with the South on the extension of slavery. If the South would not agree to respect the authority of the Constitution, then let war come. Greeley agreed with Lincoln that the Union was indestructible —and must be saved. ". . . if there must be a war, so be it!" was the *Tribune's* thundering reply. "Sumter is temporarily lost, but Freedom is saved!" wrote Greeley. "It is hard to lose Sumter, but in losing it we have gained a united people. Long live the Republic!"

Then, on May 18, a trick of fate removed Greeley from active leadership of the *Tribune*. While chopping wood and trimming trees at his home in Chappaqua, his axe handle slipped from his hand and the blade cut an ugly gash in his knee. He was quite a long distance from the house, and the long walk back made the wound even worse. He was forced to remain at home for over a month—and to turn over the *Tribune* to his managing editor, Dana.

Dana was not satisfied with the Union's slowness in carrying the fight to the Confederacy. An army had been raised and was sitting quietly near Washington, doing nothing. Finally, the excited Dana could hold back no longer. He wanted the Union to move quickly and win the war. So, on June 26, Dana blazed across the *Tribune*'s editorial page "The Nation's War Cry!—Forward to Richmond!" In his editorials, Dana said the Confederate Congress must not be allowed to meet in Richmond on July 20, as they planned. The city must be attacked and "held by the National Army."

With the world's largest circulation, Dana's editorials could not be ignored, even by President Lincoln. Other Northern newspapers picked up the "war cry" and urged the Union army to attack. Finally, under General Irvin McDowell, Union forces began to march toward Richmond, using only about 30,000 of the 100,000 men stationed near Washington. The Confederate army waited patiently about 25 miles south of Washington at a creek called Bull Run. The two armies met on July 21, 1861, and the first great battle of the Civil War began.

There General Thomas J. Jackson won his nickname "Stonewall" when his troops did not give an inch to Union forces. When another Confederate general, Joseph E. Johnstion, counterattacked the Union army from another side, McDowell's forces were wrecked and fell back. They fled toward Washington in a panic, leaving their artillery and supplies— even their dead and wounded on the battle field. It was a quick and decisive victory for the young Confederate States of America. It taught the over-confident Union leaders that their enemy was not only willing to fight, but was able to fight. McDowell was replaced by General George B. McClellan as commander of the Army of the Potomac.

Immediately after the defeat at Bull Run, Greeley and the *Tribune* were severely criticized for starting the whole affair. It was almost too much for Greeley to bear. In an editorial called "Just Once," he explained that the "war cry" had not been his own idea—and that it had certainly not been his decision—or the *Tribune*'s—to send the Union forces into battle.

The war dragged on through 1861 without much activity. The South was content to fight only on the defense, forcing the North to fight the war on unfamiliar ground. For its part, the North was trying to recover from the hard blow it received at Bull Run. The damage to the North was much worse than the loss of a battle. Its spirit was low—lower than it had ever been before. Even Greeley wrote a gloomy letter to President Lincoln, wondering if the Union cause was lost. The editor knew, however, that he could not put his fears in the editorial columns of the *Tribune*. Day after day, month after month, Greeley's *Tribune* was the firmest supporter of Lincoln's administration.

With many publications criticizing the government for not taking a bolder stand against the rebels, Lincoln was happy to have Greeley's *Tribune* on his side. "Having him firmly behind me will be helpful to me as any army of one hundred thousand men," Lincoln said with reference to Greeley. Late in 1861, an arrangement was made for the *Tribune* to receive important information on the government's decisions in advance of other newspapers. It was a happy arrangement for both Greeley and Lincoln. Still, as 1862 arrived, the Union forces avoided any major battles. Not only the Army, but Lincoln as well, appeared afraid to carry the fight to the Confederate forces. At last the *Tribune* voiced its unhappiness. The Union had raised a huge army, but was doing absolutely nothing to win the war and force the rebels back into the Union. Greeley estimated the cost of maintaining the army at between $2,000,-

000 and $3,000,000 a day—and nothing was being done. The new general of the Army of the Potomac, George McClellan, was hailed as a young Napoleon. If this was true, now was the time to prove it.

At last, in April of 1862, after almost a full year of war, McClellan decided to move once more toward Richmond. With an army of 100,000 well-trained men, he moved up the peninsula between the James and the York rivers. To everyone's surprise, the Confederate army immediately retreated, and the Union began to sense a great victory just ahead. By the middle of May the Union army was actually in sight of Richmond. McClellan prepared for a siege.

But then the Confederate generals forced the Union into a series of mistakes. Stonewall Jackson defeated three Union armies in the Shenandoah Valley, each of them larger than his own. He then made the Union think he was about to attack Washington, D.C. This feint prevented McDowell from bringing 40,000 more men to aid McClellan at Richmond. Instead Jackson turned to join Lee in defense of Richmond. The "Seven Days' Battle" began, with not only Jackson but J. E. B. (Jeb) Stuart's cavalry, helping Lee. It was too much for McClellan. After a month, the Union army was forced once more to fall back toward Washington. The second major effort of the United States had failed.

McClellan was replaced by General John Pope, who promptly moved once more toward Richmond. At Bull Run again, the Confederate army completely overpowered Pope's poorly prepared attack. Pope was then replaced as the Union general by McClellan.

Few people in the North paid much attention to the only

bright spot in the Union efforts. Early in 1862, a young soldier, Ulysses S. Grant scored two important victories in the West. Grant took Fort Henry on the Tennessee River and in a few days captured Fort Donelson. He moved quickly on up the Tennessee River and attacked the Confederate army at Shiloh. After two days of fighting Grant forced the rebels to retreat into Mississippi. These were encouraging victories for the Union, but the nation's attention continued to be on the battles in the East.

Meanwhile, Greeley was pressing hard for Lincoln to officially free all the slaves in the nation, North and South. True, the North was fighting to save the Union, but as Lincoln had already said, the nation could not last "half slave and half free." Greeley wrote Lincoln, promising the full support of the *Tribune* in any effort Lincoln might make toward emancipation.

Lincoln already had tried in March of 1862 to free the slaves in such border states as Maryland and Missouri. The President offered to have the federal government pay $400 for each slave that was set free. The plan was not accepted by the border states or by Congress. But Lincoln did not give up. In July he told his cabinet that he intended to make a proclamation as soon as the time was right. At the moment the war was not going well, and Lincoln felt he should wait for a Union victory, so that his proclamation would have the best possible effect.

Lincoln waited—but instead of a victory for the Union, the *Tribune* reported that Maryland had been invaded by the forces of Lee. The rebels won another decisive victory, this time on Union soil. Lee sent Jackson to prepare for a line of supply through the Shenandoah Valley. While Lee's army and

Jackson's army were separated, Union forces had a wonderful chance to cut Lee off. McClellan moved to put his army between Jackson and Lee, but once more McClellan delayed in attacking Lee, and "Stonewall" Jackson was well on his way to join Lee when the battle of Antietam began. After two days it ended with neither side winning. At least Lee was compelled to move his army back out of Maryland.

Less than a month before the Battle of Antietam, Greeley had published "The Prayer of Twenty Millions," urging President Lincoln to end slavery in the rebel and border states. As the response came in, supporting Greeley's stand, the President knew that the people favored an emancipation proclamation to end slavery in America for all time. Before Greeley's editorial, there was doubt in Lincoln's mind.

With the withdrawal of Lee's forces into Confederate territory, the time for action had arrived. Five days after the Battle of Antietam ended, the President announced that on January 1, 1863, he would proclaim freedom for every man held in slavery in all of the rebel states.

Greeley and the *Tribune* came quickly to Lincoln's side. "It is the beginning of the new life of the nation. God bless Abraham Lincoln."

Despite the North's view of Antietam as a victory, many thought McClellan should have followed the rebels across the Potomac. His delay caused his second removal in November of 1862. General Ambrose B. Burnside took over and immediately decided to show everyone that he was not like McClellan. In December he threw his army quickly into battle with Lee at Fredericksburg and cost the Union another heavy loss. Despite the defeat Lincoln kept his promise on January 1,

1863, by issuing his Emancipation Proclamation.

Burnside's career as a commanding general was ended after the battle at Fredericksburg. The military genius of Lee had been too much for McDowell, McClellan, Pope, McClellan once more, and now Burnside. Obviously the Union desperately needed better generals. They turned to General Joseph Hooker. Carefully he planned another campaign against Richmond. By April of 1863, Hooker's army was on the march. It met the rebel forces at Chancellorsville on May 2. On May 4, the Union army had been severely beaten again. After two full years of war, the Union was still unable to take the city of Richmond.

Spirit in the North was low, but Greeley continued to support the President throughout the dark days of defeat. Few men in the North paid much attention to the success Grant was having in the West. The fighting in the East was closer to home, and therefore more frightening. But the amazing Grant pushed on into Mississippi, approaching the important southern city of Vicksburg. Other Union forces took New Orleans and then moved up the Mississippi River and occupied Memphis. If Grant could take Vicksburg, the North would control the entire Mississippi River.

If the North was unaware of the opportunity, Lee was not. As Grant moved toward Vicksburg, Lee decided to invade Pennsylvania, hoping to draw the Union forces away from the South. At Gettysburg a Union army under General George G. Meade met Lee's forces, and after three days of furious battle, the Union forces were victorious. Badly weakened, Lee retreated into Virginia on July 4, 1863.

On the same day Grant took Vicksburg. So, with two

great victories the tide of the war began to change. The Confederates were limited in manpower, and the heavy expense of war was beginning to be a burden. Short of supplies, weapons and ammunition, the Confederates were forced to rely on the brilliance of their master-general, Lee. It was not enough.

Union armies concentrated on winning in the East. In the fall of 1863 they attacked General Bragg near Nashville. After several days, he fell back to Chattanooga. Briefly the rebels won the first few skirmishes, but Grant arrived from Vicksburg. It was too much for the Confederates. They were defeated at Chattanooga, at Lookout Mountain, again at Missionary Ridge, and at last were forced to fall back into Georgia.

All the victories of the Confederates as well as of the Union were reported with great accuracy by the New York *Tribune*. Only on the editorial page did Greeley allow his feelings to show. There, he continued his support of Lincoln's administration with all the usual Greeley enthusiasm. At least once, Greeley's support of Lincoln almost cost the *Tribune* editor his life.

In the spring of 1863, Congress passed a law drafting all able-bodied men between the ages of 20 and 45. Greeley supported the law in his editorials. When riots broke out in New York City after the first draft calls in July, one of the first places attacked was Greeley's newspaper. In the first raid the rioters smashed into the offices on the first floor, broke up the furniture, and set fire to all papers they could find. The police finally stopped the riot before anyone was seriously hurt. During a second attempt, the rioters were run off before they could enter the building.

Greeley received many threats to his life—so many, in

The editor walked through the mob as if it were not there.

fact, that a driver refused to take the editor to his office for fear they would not make it alive. Still, Greeley went on, walking through the angry mobs as if they were not even there. Shocked, they did nothing to him. The *Tribune*'s editor went about his daily work as if nothing had ever happened. The stories of Greeley's courage in the face of the angry rioters swept over the city. Some of his enemies tried to turn the story around, saying that Greeley had run from the scene in fear. But too many people had seen him going about his business with no fear at all. The rumors died out and Horace Greeley's fame was even greater.

Soon after the draft riots ended, a Hartford, Connecticut, publisher asked Greeley to begin writing a history of the Civil War. To do this while he performed his duties as editor and publisher of the *Tribune* would be a tremendous task. Greeley accepted the offer, however, and began writing *The American Conflict* in August of 1863. The first volume of 600 pages was published on April 10, 1864, the 23rd birthday of the New York *Tribune*. Writing such a long book in such a short time kept Greeley busy from ten in the morning until five in the afternoon. Still, he continued to edit his newspaper and look after his beloved farm at Chappaqua. It was, indeed, a busy year.

The spring of 1864 brought the North a new commanding general whose campaigns in the remainder of the war would be described in Greeley's next volume of *The American Conflict*. The general was Grant, who assumed command of all the Union armies. Under him, the Union moved again toward Richmond. Once more the Union troops were held off when the rebels stopped Grant's army at Petersburg.

During the summer, Greeley became involved in one of the most unusual negotiations of the war, the Niagara Peace Episode. Some of the most famous men of the time—Greeley, Lincoln, and Davis—were involved in it.

Even though Grant was having more success than the Union had ever known, the North was still eager for peace. Especially in the West and Northwest, the general feeling was that Lincoln was dragging the war out far too long. Also, many felt that his demands for ending slavery in the South were too hard.

Davis and other Confederate leaders knew of this dissatisfaction and sensed an opportunity to make the most of it to end the war on their own terms. Davis knew his army could not last much longer against Grant, and he was willing to try anything to save the Confederacy. So, he sent three men to Niagara Falls—on the Canadian side—to encourage the "peace movement" in the North. They hoped to stir up a quarrel and make the West break away from the East to form a new "western confederacy." They also hoped the "Peace Democrats" could gain control of the Democratic convention later in the year and then elect a new President of the United States who would end the war and recognize the independence of the Confederacy.

Unfortunately for the success of the scheme, Greeley got wind of it soon after the Confederate representatives arrived in Niagara. He also learned that the Confederates were already in touch with the Northern Democrats. Instantly, Greeley knew that it would be very bad for the Republican party if the Democrats should be thus responsible for ending the war. He decided Lincoln should be told of the peace talks.

Lincoln replied, telling Greeley to go to Niagara for a talk with the Confederate "ambassadors." He told Greeley to provide safe passage for them to Washington, but only if they had written proof from Davis that they truly represented the Confederacy. Lincoln also insisted that peace would have to be based on the ending of slavery and the return of the Southern states to the Union.

From the International Hotel on the United States side of Niagara, Greeley, as the representative of the President of the United States, sent word that the President would give them safe-conduct to Washington if they had the proper proof from Davis that they were really seeking a peaceful end to the war.

Nothing could have shocked the Confederates in Canada more, for they were really saboteurs carefully trying to set up a quick victory for the South. When they received Greeley's note, they were forced to admit they had nothing in writing from Davis. But, they said, if safe conduct were provided to Richmond, the proper papers could be obtained.

Greeley passed this word to Lincoln in Washington. The President repeated to Greeley his orginal conditions. The Confederates, of course, refused the offer, for peace on Lincoln's terms was the furthest thing from their mind. The whole episode was disclosed as a Confederate scheme to divide the Union.

During the following weeks, the Confederates tried to claim that Lincoln had double-crossed them by his demands. There was much criticism in the South of Lincoln's attitude. In New York, the other newspapers attacked Greeley for his part in the phony "peace episode."

If Greeley had not followed up the rumor that the saboteurs were trying to end the war peacefully, they might very well have succeeded in their plan to split the Union and win the peace for the South. Greeley's trip to Niagara ended Davis' chances of saving the Confederate States in this way.

Soon after the Niagara Peace Episode, Greeley and the rest of the North turned to the business of electing a President. Many in the North wanted to see the war ended quickly. They blamed Lincoln because the war had lasted for more than three long years. The editors of many Republican papers became worried about the coming election. Raymond of the *Times,* Weed of the Albany *Journal,* and even Greeley began to doubt that Lincoln could be re-elected to the Presidency. The great Rail-Splitter said: "Perhaps some other man may do better than I. That is probable; but I am here and that other man is not."

Lincoln got the re-nomination. Despite Greeley's early fear of running Lincoln again, the *Tribune* came out with strong support for his bid for a second term. The Democrats nominated McClellan, who favored a quick peace with the South—perhaps even with the continuation of slavery. Even with much feeling in McClellan's favor, the *Tribune* reacted with all its heaviest guns. "We MUST re-elect him," said Greeley of Lincoln, "And, God helping us, we WILL." In another blast at the Democrats, Greeley said Lee's army cheered wildly when they received the news that McClellan had been nominated by the Democrats. Still, the war dragged on, and Lincoln's chances of winning did not look good.

Soon, however, the situation began to change. Sherman took Atlanta and started his march toward Savannah and the sea. No army opposed him as he marched through Georgia.

On other battlegrounds, Sheridan was winning in the Shenandoah Valley of Virginia and Grant was valiantly carrying the fight to Lee.

The North lost heavily in Grant's attacks on Lee, but more men came to take their place. Grant continued the heavy attack, forcing Lee back toward Richmond. Suddenly, the spirit of the North was changed from defeat to victory. Lincoln no longer was being criticized, and Greeley could see the first signs of Lincoln's re-election.

The people returned Lincoln to the White House for another four-year term of office. In the *Tribune* Greeley greeted the election as a victory for freedom. The people's decision, said the *Tribune,* was that the nation would live, and slavery die.

The Union continued to win, even though the Confederate armies moved with speed and skill, dodging the Union forces for the most part, striking only when the situation was just right.

Everyone in the North and the South knew that the end was approaching. Southern troops could hardly be called armies, so poorly fed, clothed and equipped were they. Union troops, on the other hand, were fresh and ready to fight. Only the military genius of Lee held the Union from decisive victory. Greeley saw that the end of the war was near, and he began to consider how the nation could once more be united. His thoughts turned again to an old and favorite subject: creating a United States that was truly one nation, from the Atlantic to the Pacific, the South as well as the North.

Greeley discovered that Lincoln shared most of his views on "reconstruction" of the Union. Lincoln intended to bring the country together as quickly as possible after slavery was ended. He intended to restore the Southern states to their rightful position in the Union. Lincoln never lost sight of the purpose of the conflict: to save the Union and prove that it could never be destroyed by a handful of unhappy states. His attitude was forgiving, and the South would have found in him a true and understanding friend.

In March of 1865, Greeley visited Lincoln in the White House. They talked about the hard times of the war and the good times they both hoped were just ahead. On this, the two men agreed: that the Southern states were to be brought back quickly. Many powerful men in the North wanted to see the South punished severely, and Lincoln knew he would have a difficult time in getting his kind of reconstruction put through Congress. It was good to know, therefore, that the nation's largest and most powerful newspaper was standing firmly beside him. The two men had disagreed often during Lincoln's Presidency, and Greeley had always been honest enough to print his criticisms of Lincoln in the *Tribune*. On all the major issues of the war, however, Greeley had been one of Lincoln's best supporters.

This was the last meeting Greeley ever had with Lincoln. Greeley wrote later that Lincoln's face was "haggard with care and seamed with thought and trouble. . . . Judging from that scarred, rugged countenance, I do not believe that he could have lived out his second term . . . . the sunset of life was plainly looking out of his kindly eyes."

During April, Grant pushed Lee even nearer to Richmond. Then in a bold move Grant cut Lee's army from Johnston's. Lee tried to escape, but Grant blocked all lines of retreat.

Lee realized that to continue fighting would only bring more hardship on his exhausted men, and on April 9, 1865, he surrendered his army to Grant at Appomattox Courthouse, Virginia. By May 26, the last of the Confederates west of the Mississippi had also surrendered, bringing to an end the Confederate States of America.

The time for reconstruction had arrived. But shortly after the death of the Confederacy, both the North and the South suffered the worst blow of the entire war. Abraham Lincoln, who dreamed along with Greeley of a united nation, was shot by a fanatic, John Wilkes Booth, on April 14 at Ford's Theatre in Washington. The President died the next day, leaving the nation without its great leader at a time when his wisdom and patience were needed most.

A few men carried on Lincoln's work. Greeley's was one of the strongest voices in the country urging the nation to accept the Southern states back into the Union. He argued against the execution of Jefferson Davis or any man who had been involved in the Confederate cause. Few listened in the North. The war had been won—and the New York *Times* said that Jeff Davis "should be hung."

After Lincoln's death the bloodthirsty screams became even louder. A reward of $100,000 was offered for the arrest of Jefferson Davis. With Lincoln dead, the shout went up throughout the North for the life of Davis. Greeley's plea for mercy not only fell on deaf ears, it also cost the *Tribune* much circulation. Sales of his book, *The American Conflict,* dropped off sharply, and he found himself standing almost alone in his belief that the bitterness of the war should be put aside.

To Greeley, there was a far greater destiny for the United

States than to be torn apart forever in hatred between the North and the South. To heal the awful wounds of the war would not be an easy task. With cries of hatred from both North and South ringing in his ears, Greeley took on this task of rebuilding the nation.

Chapter 17

Reconstruction

A ndrew Johnson of Tennessee became President of the United States on April 15, 1865. Only a few months before, he had been elected to the vice-presidency as Lincoln's personal choice. Despite this, no man ever came to the White House with less popular or Congressional support. He was disliked in the North because he was a Southerner. He was disliked in the South because he refused to support the Confederacy. Because he was a lifelong Democrat, the Republicans could not accept him as Lincoln's true successor. The Democrats of the nation could not forgive his support of Lincoln.

Greeley was pleased when the new President announced his plans for reconstruction. Johnson told Congress in December that the time for military rule in the South was ended. He urged that the nation become "once more a united people." Greeley praised Johnson's speech to Congress in editorials, laying Greeley open to even more criticism for his "soft" policy.

Even more criticism was to come. Throughout 1865 and 1866, Jefferson Davis, had been held in jail at Fort Monroe. There had been a great deal of talk about putting Davis on trial for treason, but there had been no action. Some feared that if Davis were tried, he might be set free. So he was merely kept in prison. In January of 1866, Greeley made it plain where he stood. In the *Tribune,* he wrote that it was a farce to keep Davis in jail any longer. Varina Davis, his wife, read these remarks and wrote Greeley several letters, begging him to help free her husband.

His curiosity aroused, Greeley investigated to find out if Davis had been involved in the assassination of Lincoln or in the mistreatment of Union prisoners of war in rebel prisons. When he was satisfied that Davis was innocent of these actions, the *Tribune* started a campaign to do something about the situation. At least, wrote Greeley, Davis should be allowed to leave prison on bail. Others took up the cry as the *Tribune's* editorials stirred the conscience of the nation. In August, 1866, Gerrit Smith, one of the Confederacy's bitterest enemies, wrote President Johnson, pointing out that "Davis' long confinement without trial is an insult to the South and a dishonor to our government. There are many men who opposed slavery . . . who would eagerly go his bail. I am one of them."

Greeley continued to demand that Davis either be brought to trial or set free on bail. He reminded the country that Davis was, in a way, the representative of 6,000,000 Americans. Still, nothing was done. The *Tribune,* powerful though it was, could not move the government to action. Seeing this, Greeley decided to take matters into his own hands.

He hired an attorney, George Shea, to get Davis free on

Greeley and Jefferson Davis shook hands after bail was made.

bail. Shea finally got the U.S. Circuit Court in Richmond to agree to accept a $100,000 bond. Greeley arranged for several others to join him as bondsmen, among them Gerrit Smith and Commodore Cornelius Vanderbilt. The group traveled to Richmond in May.

With Greeley as the acknowledged leader, the bondsmen stepped forward one by one and signed their names. When it was all over and Davis was freed from jail, he came quickly to Greeley and shook his hand. It was the last time the two men ever met. Greeley had once more proved with decisive action the sincerity of his words.

Before and during the war, Greeley had been one of the South's most unpopular foes. Now Southerners saw him as a true friend. They realized this was not because Greeley had changed in any way, for he had not. He loved the South because it was a very large and important part of the United States, just as he loved the West, the North, and his native New England. When he shook Jefferson Davis' hand, it was an act of friendship that he hoped everyone would understand.

Lincoln would have understood Greeley's act in Richmond for what it was, but when the editor returned to New York City he was greeted by more criticism than he had ever before known. It was even written that the country now had a man who was more unpopular than Jefferson Davis. That man was Horace Greeley.

Circulation of the *Weekly Tribune* sank dangerously low and sales of the second volume of *The American Conflict* stopped completely. The Union League Club, of which Greeley was a member, called a special meeting to ask Greeley to explain his action. There was even a hint that his membership might be withdrawn.

As much as anything else, this insult from the Union League Club drew down the wrath of the nation's most famous editor. He answered their request for a special meeting with a letter which he also published in the *Tribune*.

"I do not recognize you as capable of judging . . . me," Greeley began. "You evidently regard me as a weak sentimentalist . . . . I arraign you as narrow-minded blockheads . . . .

[*168*]

" . . . Understand, once for all, that I dare you and defy you . . . . So long as any man was seeking to overthrow our Government, he was my enemy; from the hour in which he laid down his arms, he was my formerly erring countryman."

More than any other words following the Civil War, these explained how forgiveness is made to work for mankind. Nothing that Greeley ever did underlines his greatness so clearly as his bailing of Jefferson Davis. A storm of personal criticism and abuse in the other newspapers followed. The action cost him dearly in the North as he was accused of being a traitor to the cause he pretended to love. His critics did not understand. All of this Greeley accepted without complaint, for he was set on helping to reconstruct a united nation.

In the South, people began to realize what such men as Clay, Greeley, and Lincoln had meant for these many years when they had said the Union was indestructible.

In 1867, Greeley found little to encourage him in his struggle to restore the Union. Congress was locked in a bitter fight with President Johnson. During February of 1868, Greeley left New York for a lecture tour in some of the western states. While he was gone, the *Tribune* was under the control of its managing editor, John Russell Young. At the time, Greeley trusted Young's judgment, although he would have preferred to leave the *Tribune* in the care of his old associate, Charles A. Dana. Dana had left the paper during the war, however, to become the assistant secretary of war under Lincoln, and had gone out on his own after the war. Young was the second man who tried to do the great job that Dana had done so well.

[*169*]

While Greeley was touring, President Johnson removed Edwin Stanton as Secretary of War. Congress immediately began to talk of impeachment. In the *Tribune,* Young's editorials joined in the attack. Greeley returned to find that his own newspaper was in the middle of a campaign to have the President impeached and thrown out of office. It was a delicate situation. He did not fundamentally agree with Young's editorials, but he could hardly afford to change the newspaper's policy on Johnson over night.

It was already too late for the impeachment to be stopped; Greeley was forced to let Young continue the course established while the editor was in the West. A correspondent of the New York *World* said that on "good authority" he knew the *Tribune* would have been much milder if Greeley had been in charge at the time. In defense of his own managing editor, Greeley denied that the *Tribune* had gone astray while he was out of town. But everyone who knew Greeley knew what his feelings were in the matter.

The impeachment of Johnson failed in March, and the nation turned its attention to the election of a new President in the fall. Ulysses S. Grant was being boomed across the land. The same military glory that had earlier swept Harrison and Taylor into office was now beginning to work for the Hero of Appomattox. A little sadly, Horace Greeley gave Grant the *Tribune's* support, only when it was obvious no other Republican candidate could win. Greeley never felt that a military background was right for a career in politics.

But the *Tribune's* support was not very strong. Greeley still felt that the Republican party was best for the nation, and he supported Grant because he was the Republican nominee.

In his editorials, however, he emphasized most the election of a big Republican majority in Congress—even reminding his readers that this was especially important since Grant was not a great leader. Certainly, this was the mildest political support Greeley had ever offered. He went even further. In another slap at the Hero of Appomattox, Greeley suggested that the Democratic party should nominate Chief Justice Edward P. Chase as its candidate. Greeley pointed out that the Republicans had overlooked a very good man in him, and that Chase would be the best candidate the Democrats could find.

Even though Greeley was not at all enthusiastic about Grant as President, he worked hard for the Republican ticket. In New York State alone, the *Tribune* editor was largely responsible for raising $150,000 to meet campaign expenses. He arranged for pamphlets to be written that would attract the votes of Southern Negroes. In addition, he made as many campaign speeches as he could in support of all Republicans, including Grant. The *Weekly Tribune* recovered all the circulation lost during the Jefferson Davis affair, reaching 240,000. Editorials in every issue urged the election of Republican congressmen and senators in all states. The mighty daily *Tribune* attacked the Democratic nominees of New York City with all of its usual great vigor. Clearly, Horace Greeley did not let his feelings toward Grant interfere with his support of the Republican party.

At the same time, Greeley was also trying to make still more improvements in his now famous newspaper. His staff was still the finest in the country, and he was continuing his policy of providing space for unknown writers who would later prove to be great. Greeley made room in the *Tribune's* columns for another new writer who signed himself "Mark Twain." Some of Twain's reports to the *Tribune* in the late 1860's from foreign countries were the basis of a book called *The Innocents Abroad*. Twain acknowledged Greeley's help when he said the *Tribune's* white-haired editor had given him his "first notoriety." A great and lasting friendship developed between Twain and Greeley—just as before such men as Charles Dickens and Henry David Thoreau had been drawn to the great editor.

This was a different world from the "boiling sea of politics," and it was the world Greeley loved best. It was the sort of thing such old associates as Weed and Seward could never understand. To Greeley these were the things that mattered most. He wanted the best men possible to write for the *Tribune* —and usually he got them. It made the *Tribune* the great newspaper it was. Greeley searched always for new talent, and in 1868 the editor was determined to bring into the *Tribune* a man he had been watching for several years. His name was Whitelaw Reid.

Finally, in September, Greeley persuaded Reid to come to New York from his Cincinnati paper. For years, Greeley had missed the steady business mind of his first partner, Thomas McElrath. Further, he had missed the brilliance of Dana, who was the *Tribune's*—and journalism's—first managing editor. In Reid, Greeley saw a great combination of Dana and Mc-Elrath. He did not give up in his determination to have Reid on the *Tribune* with him. When Reid finally decided to come, Greeley named him the "first writing editor," subject only to himself and Young.

Thus Reid came to the *Tribune* in time to see come into

the newspaper's office the results of the national election that made Ulysses S. Grant President in a landslide victory for the Republican party. During the remainder of 1868 and the early days of 1869, Reid proved the trust Greeley had shown in hiring him. By summer Young had resigned as managing editor, and Reid was immediately appointed to the vacant position.

Reid was the last of Greeley's famous assistants. Starting with Raymond, then Dana and followed by Sidney Howard Gay and John Russell Young, the *Tribune's* list of assistants was a catalog of the great journalists of the day. Some of Greeley's enemies claimed that without these great assistants, the *Tribune* would never have grown to its enormous power in the nation. Each of these men, however, admitted that Greeley was always the one final voice in *Tribune* policies. Even after they were gone from Greeley's paper, they continued to respect their former boss. Raymond feuded with Greeley often —was even one of Greeley's bitterest enemies—but he was the first to admit that Greeley had decided the course of his life. After Dana became the editor of the *Sun,* he still kept a picture of Greeley over his desk. Whitelaw Reid said, "I feel more comfortable when . . . I can get to you for advice or counsel."

With the election of Grant and the hiring of Reid as first writing editor, Greeley was ready to return to calmer days. His paper was strengthened to a greatness it had never seen before, and its budget for a single year now was $1,000,000. Stock in the company was more valuable than ever, and its owners were making more money than ever. But surprisingly enough, the founder was not among those who enjoyed the immense

[*173*]

profits from its success. For Greeley had sold all of his original fifty shares of stock but nine! The legal ownership of the *Tribune* had passed from its founder. Yet no one doubted that the newspaper was "Greeley's *Tribune*"—and many actually felt that the newspaper would collapse into nothing if its famed editor should ever retire.

One young man Greeley hired in 1870 was Joseph Bishop. As so many had before him, Bishop rose in the newspaper profession, becoming an editorialist of the New York *Evening Post*. In *Notes and Anecdotes of Many Years* Bishop described exactly what the *Tribune* was like in those days of almost unbelievable greatness:

"The editorial room fronted on Printing House Square and was entered through the reporters' room . . . . [The reporters] regarded the front room as the very heaven of their aspirations. They looked with admiration and envy upon the men—George Ripley, Whitelaw Reid, Bayard Taylor, William Winter and John Hay—who walked daily through the city room into it. For, ill-furnished and ill-kept as 'The Tribune' office was in those days, it harbored a moral and intellectual spirit that I met nowhere else during my thirty-five years of journalistic experiences.

"Every member of the force, from reporter to editor, regarded it a great privilege to be on 'The Tribune' and to write for its columns, and that there could be no higher ambition than to write for the same page as that . . . for which Horace Greeley wrote. All the reporters who were ambitious studied that page with care daily seeking to fit themselves to write ultimately for it.

"The quaintest figure in the place was that of the great editor, Horace Greeley, careless and dishevelled in dress as if he had put his clothes on in the dark, with the round and rosy face of a child and cherubic expression of simplicity and gentleness. At the time of which I am speaking he occupied a small room on the second floor of the building, access to which was by means of an iron stairway from the counting room.

" 'The Tribune' was a tremendous force in the country because of the personal faith of the plain people in the honesty of its editor. Every word 'The Tribune' printed was believed implicitly because he was the man behind it.

"The power that he wielded was not equaled by any editor of his time—neither has it been equaled by any editor since."

That last statement is as true now as it was when Bishop wrote it. There have been many great editors and great newspapers—but none ever held the tremendous respect and influence that was the *Tribune's* in its Greeley days.

This is not to say that Greeley had no enemies, for he had many. Even his direst foe, however, knew that what the *Tribune* printed in its news columns was as near the truth of what happened as human beings could make it. If they wished to disagree with the editorials signed "H. G.," this was all right with the editor. He kept the editorial page his personal property. On it, he expressed whatever he thought; and for the most part the people of America agreed with him. More than that, Greeley became, in a sense, the conscience of his time. He became a familiar sight on the Pacific Coast as well as the Atlantic. He traveled through the West, the North, and the South until his shambling country walk, the hat cocked on the back of his head, the famous white coat and heavy boots were as familiar

[*175*]

in far-away Houston as they were in New York itself.
Horace Greeley became a legend.

Chapter 18

The Battle for Peace

G rant had not been President much over a year when many Republicans began to suspect that he was a far better soldier than he was a statesman. General Grant had been more than liberal and kind with the defeated armies of the Confederacy. At Appomattox he allowed the Southern soldiers to keep their pistols and suggested they even keep their horses for the spring plowing. President Grant, however, seemed to be a different sort of man. He began to sympathize with the "radical" Republican leaders who wanted to continue indefinitely the domination of the Southern states—the same group that eagerly had tried to throw Johnson out of the White House. Despite the obvious readiness of the South to govern itself once more, Grant continued to support the carpetbaggers and scalawags who were attempting to keep control in the Southern states.

Greeley had never been one of Grant's admirers off the

battlefield, but he was willing to give the President a chance. When the criticism began, Greeley admitted "we have had greater Presidents than Grant, but scarcely one who deserved the running fire of . . . fault-finding to which he has been subjected." Greeley went on to warn that Grant's critics were doing more than injuring the President—they were "in fact undermining the Republican party."

Privately, Greeley felt that Grant was not a satisfactory President, and he slowly began to join the other newspapers in their criticisms. In the *Tribune,* he made it plain that he was in favor of Southern efforts to promote industry. He disagreed completely with Grant's policy of keeping the South under the heavy thumb of Northern industrial power.

Greeley's friendly attitude toward the South was quickly recognized and he was asked in 1871 to speak at the Texas state fair in Houston. When the word spread that the famous editor was to speak there, other cities asked him to visit them. He spoke in Houston, New Orleans, Galveston and Vicksburg.

In each, the famous journalist showed his usual courage in criticizing such race baiting organizations as the Ku Klux Klan. He impatiently reminded his Southern audiences that they should have a more constructive attitude toward Negroes. On the other hand, he praised the way the Southern states were resuming their responsible positions in the nation. He praised the economic growth he found in the South and viciously attacked the presence of Northern carpetbaggers. Most of all, Greeley urged his audiences toward greater national unity. That the Mississippi should run through two separate nations, Greeley said, was unthinkable.

[*178*]

He reminded the Southern people that they were just as much Americans as anyone in the North. At Vicksburg, Greeley told his audience that he looked forward to the time when Lee and Stonewall Jackson would be recognized throughout the North for the great men they were, and to the time when in the South such men as Lincoln, Grant, and Sheridan would also be recognized for their greatness. Above all, the unity of America was the thing Horace Greeley sought to build in his trip to the South. He was honest in his criticism as well as in his praise. His trip was a magnificent succeess.

When he returned, Greeley found a huge reception waiting for him in the Lincoln Club at Union Square. The walls were decorated with large photographs of him, along with flowers and the flag of the United States. To Greeley's surprise, rumors were flying that he should be a candidate for President in 1872.

For the occasion Greeley put aside his famed white coat and heavy boots. He actually wore evening clothes to the reception—one of the few times that he was ever seen in formal dress. It was a grand and happy time for Greeley. But even more was to come.

Outside, on Union Square, a platform had been built and several thousand New Yorkers clamored around it, waiting for Greeley to make a speech. Late in the night, he appeared and mounted the platform with the applause and cheers of the crowd ringing in his ears. As he looked at the people around him, he realized they were not waiting for just another speech from a well-known newspaper editor. They were waiting for leadership from a man they thought might pull the nation together and make it move forward once more. Greeley looked

[*179*]

In Union Square as in the South, Greeley pleaded for unity.

out over the expectant faces, gathering his thoughts.

When he began, his voice was calm. He explained the purpose of his trip to the South. He had wanted to make everyone understand "that we are all Americans." He told the people in Union Square how he had hoped in Vicksburg for the day when the South would honor Grant. He repeated that he hoped the day would also come when the North—even New York City—would honor Lee. "Possibly you are not willing to go so far as that," Greeley said. "Very well, then, there is no hurry. Take your time; I can wait. I can wait!"

Greeley paused, seeing that his tough words were slowly sinking into the consciences of his listeners. Then he did something most unusual—he shook off the first of the many chains of party affiliation. For many years, Greeley had been identified as a Whig leader, and he had been one of the earliest and most important organizers of the Republican party. Now, with Grant's administration following a policy of slow reconstruction in the South, Greeley could no longer ignore what he believed were bad mistakes in Republican policy. Personally, Greeley said, he was weary of the drawn-out reconstruction in the South. No matter whether Democrats and Republicans were in agreement or disagreement—the important thing was for both parties to "promote the prosperity, the happiness and true glory of the American people."

Greeley's audience applauded enthusiastically. Suddenly, Greeley—a man important in Presidential campaigns for 30 years—found himself cast in a new and gigantic role. He was himself moving to the front as a candidate for the nation's highest office.

Greeley had risen to the peak of the newspaper profession. More than that, he had become one of the two or three most famous men in America. That night in Union Square brought even a greater measure of fame and prestige. Yet, when the crowd had moved away, it left behind a lonely man, feeling a little out of place in this new role. He looked down at the formal evening clothes he wore and remembered the awful poverty of his childhood. He was in his 60's now; and if the road of life had led him far from the log hut of West Haven, the journey had also been perhaps too fast. For much of life had passed him by.

As much as anything, Greeley had always wanted a home. But this he had never had with Mary. As the years passed, she became increasingly obsessed with her health. She spent most of her time in search of a doctor who might cure her imaginary ills. At home, she spent most of her time in bed. She made frequent trips abroad to consult with foreign specialists. She was gone much of the time from Chappaqua, taking their two daughters with her and leaving her husband in the cold and empty loneliness of a deserted house.

It was not much of a home, but still Horace Greeley loved the place deeply and spent as much of his time as he could at his "farm." He even wrote a book, *What I Know of Farming*, that was published in 1871. In it, he urged modern methods in agriculture, for he had taken "Greeley's Bog" and turned it into one of the most beautiful places in New York State.

But this was not enough. It could hardly replace his sons who had died in their childhood and the wife and daughters he had lost to so many trips from home. Greeley was left alone most of the time, to make his own way as best he could.

He never had many close friends, even among his associates at the *Tribune*. Those he did have, however, were dear to him and helped to fill the gap of his lonely life. One of the first, of course, had been Margaret Fuller. Another was Mrs. Rebekah Whipple, a lifelong friend from his childhood days in West Haven. But the last—and probably greatest—friend Greeley ever had was Mrs. Margaret Allen of Jamestown, New York.

All of Greeley's close friends were women. No man was ever able to penetrate and touch the heart of the *Tribune's* editor. He would talk with men about writing or politics or farming, but he would never talk to them about himself. He opened his heart only to those whose hearts were softer than any man's he knew.

Greeley was introduced to Mrs. Allen in 1865 by his friend, P. T. Barnum, and instantly the two began a great and close friendship. Just as he had before with Miss Fuller, Greeley wrote many letters to Mrs. Allen. They were a bursting revelation of his view of life and of himself.

"I have not many friends," Greeley wrote to Mrs. Allen in the fall of 1871. "My life has been too hurried, and too much absorbed in pressing duties and anxious cares. Of my few friends most are women and these I am proud of . . . ."

Later in November he wrote again: "I have been chopping at Chappaqua every Saturday of late, and I have a lot of red cedar cut up into firewood and well-seasoned. You know how pleasant is the odor of burning cedar. Well, I reserve this to warm and light my hearth when I can—at some future day with my family about me, go up and spend three or four consecutive evenings—long, bright evenings . . . ."

But by Christmas, 1871, Chappaqua was still lonely. "My sixtieth Christmas is going soberly and with abundance of work," Greeley wrote. "I am no richer unless in friends for my last ten or twelve years of hard work, and I begin to long for quiet and rest. I have hardly known what home meant for years and am too busy to enjoy anything. I most regret the lack of time to read books . . . ."

As the new and fateful year of 1872 began, oftentimes his letters to Mrs. Allen were written late in the cold winter night as he sat in his small and cluttered *Tribune* office, waiting for a printer's proof of the next day's editorial. When the boy delivered the proof, the editor carefully checked it for mistakes and called the copyboy by pulling the heavy bell-cord beside his desk. Then, with another long day finally ended, the great editor pulled on his heavy white coat, turned out the last light in the *Tribune* office, and stepped outside into biting cold of the New York night that seemed to swallow him up.

He pulled his hat down hard and turned up his collar against the winter wind. Behind him, the Tribune Building stood dark against the sky. But deep inside, the newspaper that he loved was going on—the typesetters making the final corrections and the pressmen making the last preparations for printing the next morning's edition. Greeley listened to the familiar sounds of the busy shop and pulled his coat a little tighter as the chilling memory of 30 years swept over him, joining and even exceeding the coldness of the night.

The great editor turned and slowly began to walk away.

Chapter 19

A Lasting Victory

As 1872 went on, Horace Greeley found his name mentioned more and more as a Presidential candidate. On every occasion he denied any interest in the honor. "Leave my name out of the question as a candidate," he wrote to a friend. But still the talk continued.

In the editorial columns of the *Tribune,* Greeley was becoming even more dissatisfied with Grant's administration. Time after time he blasted Grant's policies toward the South and its reconstruction. It appeared certain that the Republicans would renominate Grant for a second term, and the *Tribune's* editor could see no way to support Grant with honesty. He even wrote a letter to Mrs. Allen, asking what her opinions were of his abandoning Grant. Obviously, Greeley was getting closer and closer to a break with the Republican party he had helped to start.

Another cause of Greeley's growing dissatisfaction with

the Republican party was Roscoe Conkling, whose political machine had replaced that of Thurlow Weed in New York. Greeley had fought the organization of Conkling's machine from the start, but Conkling quickly received the aid of Grant through several appointments of "Conklingites" to key positions in New York State.

This was too much. Greeley turned the *Tribune's* heaviest guns on the man in the White House. He began urging that Presidents should be limited to a single term in office, and he suggested that New York political affairs should be free from outside interference. Then, in a surprising move, Greeley suggested that New York City could best be governed by a combination of the best men in the Democratic and Republican parties. Greeley offered to co-operate with his old rivals, the Democrats of Tammany Hall!

Clearly, the ties between Greeley and the regular Republicans were falling away. By March 7, 1872, the last link was gone. In the *Tribune* Greeley published a letter he had written to the chairman of the Republican National Committee, asking that his name be removed from the list of those who would be called to the national convention. Greeley explained to his readers that if he should attend the convention he would be expected to support its nominees. With Grant obviously lacking opposition, Greeley had no intention of being forced to support a man whose policies he disliked so much.

Meanwhile, Greeley was not alone in his criticism of Grant. In far-off Missouri, Republicans opposed to Grant had organized what they called the Liberal Republican party. The new group had swept to victory in the state election of 1870 and had begun to spread across the country. By 1872 the Liberal

Republicans were strong enough to make plans for a national convention of their own in Cincinnati—and for a try at electing a Liberal Republican to the Presidency.

When Greeley broke off from the regular Republican party, the Liberal Republicans saw their opportunity. Greeley had always treated the new party with fairness in the *Tribune,* agreeing with all of its principles except one. The Liberal Republicans were not in favor of a high protective tariff. When they came to invite Greeley to their Cincinnati convention, he explained that he could not support them if they were opposed to a high tariff.

So, when the convention met on May 1, Greeley remained at his desk. In his place went Whitelaw Reid, who set to work immediately to prevent the convention from including "free trade" in its platform. This was not Reid's only job. He succeeded on the tariff issue, and he succeeded too in the real purpose of his mission in Cincinnati. On May 3, he sent a one-word wire to his editor in New York City. It read: "NOMINATED."

Greeley was at his desk in the *Tribune* offices when the message was delivered. Quickly his room was crowded with editors and reporters congratulating him. Outside, a crowd was gathering in front of the Tribune Building, slowly beginning a steady chant for "Uncle Horace" to appear.

Obviously overcome, first by the telegram and then by the cheering crowd, he moved to the window and waved his hand to the people standing below. The cheering went on for at least 15 minutes. As Greeley watched at the window, he decided that if the Liberal Republicans wanted him to run, he would give it everything he had. And that—as Grant would

[*187*]

Greeley was overwhelmed by the cheers for his nomination.

soon discover—was a lot!

Greeley "clubs" sprang up almost overnight. His great following in the West and in the South was more than encouraging. To show their support, thousands in St. Louis and New Orleans began wearing white hats similar to Greeley's. In mid-May, Greeley resigned as the *Tribune's* editor until the campaign should be over. On July 9, the Greeley forces were further encouraged when the Democratic National Convention met in Baltimore, accepted and endorsed the platform of the Liberal Republicans, and offered Greeley their own nomination for the Presidency.

Also in July, Mary Greeley returned from Europe. When Horace met her ship, he discovered that his wife was seriously ill. This time it was not imaginary. She was so crippled with rheumatism that she had to be carried from the ship. He took her home to Chappaqua and spent the rest of the month trying to nurse her back to health.

By August, the Presidential campaign could no longer be set aside. In the truest Greeley manner, he hit the campaign trail in as great a campaign as any he had ever fought in the editorial columns of his newspaper. He toured New Jersey, Pennsylvania, Ohio, Kentucky, and Indiana. This was the first time in the history of the country that a Presidential candidate had campaigned like this. Only Henry Clay, before Greeley, had even gone so far as to make two short speeches. In 1872, however, Horace Greeley made many, putting his position before the voters of the nation.

In Ohio, Greeley made one of his greatest speeches. In it, he urged the people: "Let us forget that we fought. Let us remember only that we have made peace. Let us say there shall be no . . . people over whom we triumph. Our triumph is their triumph . . . . Our triumph is not the triumph of a section; it is not the triumph of a race; it is not the triumph of a class. It is the triumph of the American people, making us all, in life, in heart and purpose, the people, the one people of the great American Republic. Fellow citizens, to the work of Reconciliation I dedicate myself."

And again: "If elected," Greeley said, "I shall be the President of the whole people and not of any party. I . . . trust that the masses of the people, North and South, are eager to clasp hands across the bloody chasm which has too long divided them . . . ."

These were great and stirring words from a dedicated American. As the autumn leaves began to turn, however, Greeley's chances started to fade. The huge Republican political machine began to click, while many Northern Democrats could not forget Greeley's 30 years of opposition. When the early results came in, North Carolina, Maine and Vermont were all solidly in the Grant column. With October, even more states fell to Grant, and Greeley's defeat seemed to come closer with each new day.

Greeley returned to New York in October and found his wife's condition much worse than when he had left. Unable to move herself because of the awful pains of rheumatism, she also was now suffering from dropsy. Never a large woman, Mary Greeley lost even more weight, and Horace knew that the end of her life was near. He stayed with her constantly in their Chappaqua home, watching over her through the long nights with almost no sleep at all. When morning came, the worries of the Presidential race were added to Greeley's troubles.

To his childhood friend, Mrs. Whipple, Greeley wrote: "I am glad that the election will soon be over . . . . You must not take our reversals too seriously. I may soon have to shed tears for my wife, but shall not shed one for any possible result of the [election]."

Mary Greeley died on October 30, 1872. It was a crushing loss to her husband, for despite the imperfections of their home life, there was a deep bond of devotion between them. A few days after her death, Greeley wrote to a friend: "My house is desolate, my future dark, my heart a stone."

Within another two days the saddened and weary editor received still another tremendous blow. Grant swept to victory in the race for the Presidency of the United States. Once more the symbol of the "military hero" had been too much to over-

[*190*]

come. Horace Greeley's name joined that list which includes many great Americans who never reached the Presidency, such men as Alexander Hamilton, Benjamin Franklin, John Marshall, Daniel Webster, and Henry Clay. He was in company he need not be ashamed of.

In many ways, Greeley's showing against Grant was remarkable. The final results showed 2,834,070 Americans voted for the *Tribune's* famous editor while Grant's total was 3,597,000, giving Greeley a little over 43 per cent of all the votes in the election. (Lincoln had had less than 40 per cent in 1860.) Grant was supported by the businessmen and had the backing of a well-organized party. Greeley, on the other hand, was running on a new party's ticket and did not receive the Democrats' full support. Even so, Horace Greeley ran as close a race as many had before him. He carried 6 of the 37 states in the Union—as good as Clay had done against Jackson or Harrison when he lost to Van Buren. Greeley's record was far better than Scott's against Pierce. The greatest tribute Greeley received, however, was from the six states that voted for him, each either Southern or "border." It proved that these states—once opposed to the Union—now realized that Greeley's policy of a united nation was the surest road to greatness. The words that Greeley spoke during his trip to the South in 1871 were not forgotten by the people in 1872.

On November 8, still only days after his wife's tragic death and his defeat in the election Horace Greeley published "a card" in the New York *Tribune*. It announced that he was returning to his former post as editor after "embarking on another line of business six months ago." The burden of the past weeks, however, had been too much for Greeley. Exhausted beyond

[*191*]

any further endurance, he finally collapsed in the middle of November and was taken to a hospital at Pleasantville, New York.

As the late autumn days went by, the great editor did not respond to treatment. His body and his mind were at last worn out, the great machine finally run down. He was unconscious most of the time; but on November 29, 1872, he looked clearly at his two daughters, Ida and Gabrielle, and spoke after a moment of consideration: "It is done," he said. "I have fought the good fight. I Know that My Redeemer Liveth."

That was the end.

On Wednesday, December 4, 1872, the funeral procession of Horace Greeley moved slowly down Fifth Avenue. The guard of honor included Thurlow Weed, William Cullen Bryant, and Horatio Seymour. The Lincoln Club of New York, the Typographical Society, and the Union League Club all marched in the procession. Thousands lined the streets to pay their respects to the great editor. In addition to a notable representation of the nation's press and governors from New York and the neighboring states, President Grant, Vice-President Colfax and Chief Justice Chase were present to pay their respects.

Men whom Horace Greeley had opposed were as much in evidence as his thousands of friends. For all recognized that this was a truly amazing life. He had risen from a log hut in West Haven, Vermont, to become the greatest editor in the history of journalism and one of the most famous men in the world. Though his life was scarred by tragic defeats and loss, it had been marked by great victories.